THE DANCE

OF THE ANCIENT GREEK THEATRE

THE DANCE
OF THE
ANCIENT
GREEK
THEATRE

BY *Lillian B. Lawler*

UNIVERSITY OF IOWA PRESS Ψ IOWA CITY

Second Printing, March 1974

PREFACE

It has been my endeavor in this monograph to present for classicists, and for serious students of the Greek drama and of the history of the dance as well, a brief survey of what is known of the dances in the dramatic and cyclic performances in the Greek theatre (and particularly in the theatre at Athens); also, to discuss some of the problems in the field of the dramatic and cyclic dances; and to offer a few suggestions and interpretations in connection with various disputed aspects of the subject. I have, however, refrained from entering into the innumerable controversies which have attended all discussions of the origin of the Greek drama, and have sought wherever possible to isolate the problems of the dances from those of the drama as a whole.

Since it has been deemed inadvisable to use Greek type in the monograph, the problem of the transliteration of Greek words and titles has arisen. In practice, complete consistency seems impossible in such transliteration. Accordingly, an effort has been made to use the best-known equivalents of the titles of plays and other works—e.g., *Birds, Frogs, Ecclesiazusae, Seven against Thebes, Oedipus the King, Trojan Women, Bacchae, Hercules Furens, Dyskolos; Iliad* and *Odyssey; Laws* and *Poetics; Anabasis; Rudens.* In technical terminology such forms as *chorēgus* and *coryphaeus* have been used, but, for the less familiar terms, such forms as *kōmos, parodos, sikinnis, cheir kataprēnēs, rhiknousthai,* etc., have been adopted. The reader's indulgence is asked for these apparently planless discrepancies.

No formal bibliographies have been included, but it is hoped that the references in the notes will be helpful to readers who may wish to pursue further a study of both the dance and the drama.

Lillian B. Lawler

Iowa City, July, 1964.

102,544

CONTENTS

I | THE DANCE OF THE DITHYRAMB

The problem of the origin of the Greek drama is one that has never been solved to the complete satisfaction of the generations of scholars who have pondered over it.[1] One thing, however, seems highly probable—that all the performances which, in the genres of dithyramb, tragedy, comedy, and satyr play, were the glory of the Athenian theatre in the classical period, had their ultimate origin in primitive rituals of song and dance of one sort or another; and certainly song and dance continued to be of the greatest importance in all of them, throughout the best period of the Athenian civilization.

It seems strange to the modern student that, in spite of this orchestic wealth, there have come down to us practically no descriptions of the dances of the drama,[2] and little direct infor-

---

[1] Various theories on the origin of the Greek drama may be found in the following works: Margarete Bieber, *The History of the Greek and Roman Theater* (2nd ed.; Princeton, 1961); Peter D. Arnott, *An Introduction to the Greek Theatre* (London and New York, 1959); Gerald F. Else, *Aristotle's Poetics: The Argument* (Cambridge, Mass., 1957); Gerald F. Else, "The Origin of *Tragoedia*," *Hermes*, LXXXV (1957), 17-46; Martin P. Nilsson, "Der Ursprung der Tragödie," in his *Opuscula Selecta* (Lund, 1951), I, 61-145; Roy C. Flickinger, *The Greek Theater and Its Drama* (4th ed.; Chicago, 1936); A. W. Pickard-Cambridge, *Dithyramb, Tragedy, and Comedy* (1st ed.; Oxford, 1927; 2nd ed., revised by T. B. L. Webster; New York, 1962); Francis M. Cornford, *The Origin of Attic Comedy* (London, 1914); Sir William Ridgeway, *The Origin of Tragedy* (Cambridge, 1910); Jane E. Harrison, *Themis* (Cambridge, 1912).

[2] The concluding lines (1474-1537) of the *Wasps* of Aristophanes furnish the only apparent description which is extant, and it presents many problems of interpretation, as we shall see.

mation on their nature and appearance. Choreography and spectacle which must have been strikingly beautiful seem to have been taken more or less for granted, as being familiar to all Greeks. As a result, the modern scholar who seeks to gain some idea of the nature of the dances must piece together bits of information dropped casually by Greek writers of all periods, and fragmentary or disjointed comments by post-classical lexicographers and scholiasts who had never seen the dances and obviously had no idea what they were really like. Nevertheless, the task is not a hopeless one, for the bits of information are numerous, and in many cases they corroborate one another, and are clarified by passages in the extant plays.

A Greek writer[3] tells us that tragedy was an Athenian invention of great antiquity. Aristotle adds the information that tragedy was derived from improvisations of the "leaders (*exarchontes*) of the dithyramb"; also, that tragedy developed out of a satyric and dance-like performance.[4]

The dithyramb was a song and dance in honor of Dionysus as divinity of fertility, grapes, and wine. At the spring festival of the god it set forth, to the music of the double flute in the Phrygian mode, the story of his birth and his adventures.[5] It is said to have originated in merrymaking in the countryside and at drinking bouts.[6] The participants were men, whose condition in early times, at least, is well suggested by the old Greek saying, "When you drink water, it isn't a dithyramb";[7] and by the boast of the seventh-century poet Archilochus of Paros that he knows how to lead (*exarxai*) the dithyramb when he is "smitten with wine."[8]

We are told[9] that the dance of the dithyramb was "full of movement" (*kekinēmenos*), very "frenzied" (*enthousiōdēs*),

---

[3] Pseudo-Plato *Minos* 321 A.

[4] *Poetics* 1449 A, 9-11 and 20-24.

[5] Plato *Laws* 700 B.

[6] Proclus *Chrestomathia*, ap. Phot. *Bibl.* 320 A, 33.

[7] Epicharmus, fragment 132 Kaibel, 78 Olivieri; ap. Athenaeus 14.628 A.

[8] Fragment 77 Diehl, 77 Bergk; ap. Athenaeus 14.628 A-B. Archilochus seems to have introduced a Dionysiac cult into Paros; Webster (Pickard-Cambridge, 2nd ed.; above, note 1, p. 10) thinks he may have written and led a dithyramb for the new cult.

[9] Proclus *Chrestomathia*, ap. Phot. *Bibl.* 320 A, 33; cf. schol. on Plato *Republic* 3.394 C.

arousing feelings appropriate to the god, and that it was wild (*sesobētai*) in its rhythms. The name applied to it by the Greeks throughout its history was *tyrbasia*. The word is related to *tyrbē*, which denotes "tumult, revel, disorder, confusion," and which was, indeed, used as the name of a festival of Dionysus in the Peloponnesus.[10] Some modern scholars believe that the participants in the earliest period may have been masked and costumed as satyrs or "goat-men," the unrestrained and sportive mythical attendants of Dionysus. Men so costumed are portrayed in Dionysiac context on Greek vases; but none of the vases goes back to so early a period as that with which we are concerned.[11] A passage in the Suidas *Lexicon* (*s.v.* "Arion"), dealing with changes made in the dithyramb in the middle of the seventh century, contains the statement that at that time there were brought in "satyrs speaking in meter"; but whether the writer means that the innovation was the meter or the "satyrs" or both, or whether he is using "satyrs" figuratively, to denote merely the *choreutae*, or members of the choral group, we do not know.

The word *dithyramb* is apparently non-Greek. It has long been believed that the cult of Dionysus, in which it had a place, originated in Thrace and Phrygia, and spread thence to Greece shortly before the beginning of the historical period. However, the discovery in recent years of the name "Dionysus" on a Mycenaean tablet from Pylos has opened up the possibility that the cult, although definitely Eastern in origin, may have reached Greece first through the Minoans and Mycenaeans. As Webster has suggested,[12] it may have been *re-introduced* into the Greek cities from Thrace and Phrygia some centuries after the collapse of the Mycenaean civilization.

Nevertheless, in antiquity various Greek lands claimed title to the "invention" of the dithyramb—among them Naxos, Thebes, and Magna Graecia. The earliest extant mention of the word in Greek is in the lines of the Ionian poet Archilochus, cited above; yet the early dithyramb seems to have had its best development in the Peloponnesus, among the Dorian Greeks.

---

[10] Pausanias 2.24.6.

[11] Flickinger (above, note 1), pp. 24-25; New York, Metropolitan Museum krater (Polion), No. 25.78.66; cf. Pollux 4.118.

[12] T. B. L. Webster, *From Mycenae to Homer* (London, 1958), pp. 49-51, 293.

It is attested that in the city of Sicyon, in the Peloponnesus, there were ritual *tragikoi choroi* of great antiquity, performed annually in honor of Adrastus, a legendary king.[13] The name seems to mean "goat dances," but we do not know why these dances were so called. Some scholars have conjectured that the participants were costumed as daemons, half human, half animal in form; others, that the performers encircled a sacrificial goat; still others, that the goat was a prize in a song-and-dance competition. In about 590 B.C. the "goat choruses" were transferred from the cult of the hero Adrastus to that of the god Dionysus. The term *tragikoi choroi*, used in connection with these performances, seems to have been borrowed by other cities.

Among the Ionian Greeks, the mythological attendants of Dionysus were generally thought of not as "goat-men" but as "horse-men," or *sileni*. In Ionian art these attendants are usually represented as old men with horses' ears, tails, and hoofs. Again we do not know whether the artists are portraying purely mythological creatures, or men costumed as *sileni*, performing dances in honor of Dionysus. Later, in Athenian art, we find creatures which are combinations of satyrs and *sileni*.[14]

In any case, there seems to be some possibility that one element, at least, in the origin and development of the dance of the dithyramb was animal mummery.[15] Such mummery was common in prehistoric times all around the shores of the Mediterranean— and indeed is found among most primitive peoples, even to this day.

Archilochus speaks particularly of "leading" the dithyramb, and we recall Aristotle's specific mention of *exarchontes* of the same song and dance. In the *Bacchae* of Euripides (line 140) Dionysus himself is referred to as *exarchos* of a ritual dance. The

---

[13] Herodotus 5.67.
[14] Flickinger (above, note 1), p.29.
[15] Cf. A. B. Cook, *Zeus* (Cambridge, 1914-1940), I, 665-715; particularly 702-705 with Plate XXXVIII. Cf. also the "chorus" of animal-headed women on the famed Lycosura drapery found at a shrine of Despoina—Guy Dickins, "Damophon of Messene," *Annual of the British School at Athens*, XIII (1906-1907), 392-395 and Plate XIV; Guy Dickins, *Hellenistic Sculpture* (Oxford, 1920), p. 62 and Fig. 48; A. W. Lawrence, *Later Greek Sculpture* (London, 1927), Plate LV. Pickard-Cambridge (1st ed.; above, note 1, pp. 50 and 133, and 2nd ed., above, note 1, pp. 112-124) discusses this subject at some length.

usage calls to mind two passages in the epic poems,[16] both descriptions of dances, in each of which two tumblers, acting as "leaders," whirl among the dancers. (Tumbling in time to music, of course, was regarded as a form of dance in antiquity.) Even in modern times we find a leader, or two leaders, in many of the folk dances of the Greek people. Keeping within the general framework of the dance rhythm, the leader breaks away from his companions at frequent intervals, and executes a brilliant array of steps, variations, and acrobatics, on his own initiative.[17] It is likely that the leader of the dithyramb in Archilochus' day, when "smitten" with wine, may have engaged in antics of a similar nature, to the loud shouts of onlookers and fellow dancers. We may assume that the whole performance was something of a joyous, drunken rout, with aimless and wandering steps, uncouth gestures, horseplay, and loud, largely extemporized ejaculations in honor of Dionysus, in prose or verse or both.

We have testimony that at some time after the middle of the seventh century B.C., Arion of Lesbos, then a visitor at the court of Periander in Corinth, made notable changes in the dithyramb as performed in that city. Herodotus (1.23) says that Arion "poetized"[18] the dithyramb, "gave it a name," and "taught" (i.e., produced) it at Corinth. The Suidas *Lexicon* (*s.v.* "Arion") states that Arion invented the *tragikos tropos* (perhaps the musical mode afterwards customarily used in the dithyramb); was the first to "set" the chorus; sang a dithyramb; gave a name to that which was sung by the chorus; and introduced "satyrs speak-

---

[16] *Iliad* 18.604-606; *Odyssey* 4.18-19. In these passages many editors, following the discussion in Athenaeus 5.180 D-E, adopt the reading *exarchontos* instead of *exarchontes* and refer the word to *molpēs*, "song," instead of to the tumblers; others keep the reading *exarchontes*, and refer it to the tumblers. The verb *exarchō* and the noun *exarchos* are used in several passages in Greek literature to refer to the leader of a choral song, sung with or without an accompanying dance or procession, or to the leader of group action—cf. *Iliad* 18.51 and 316; 24.720-722; Xenophon, *Anab.* 5.4.14; *Cyrop.* 3.3.58; Pausanias 5.18.4.

[17] In general it is not safe to draw conclusions from modern Greek dances and apply them indiscriminately to ancient dances; however, in this case the similarity is probably significant. For a different interpretation of the Aristotelian passage mentioned in this paragraph see Gerald F. Else, *Aristotle's Poetics* (above, note 1), pp. 156-163.

[18] This is Flickinger's translation (above, note 1), pp. 8-10, of *poiēsanta*. Cf. Plato *Rep.* 3.394 C.

[5]

ing in meter." Proclus (above, note 6) seems to imply that it was Arion who gave to the dithyrambic dance its characteristically circular form, with movement around the altar of Dionysus. It is generally believed that Arion wrote good lyrics for the dithyrambic *choreutae*, composed music for the lyrics, taught the *choreutae* some appropriate dance steps and gestures, rehearsed them carefully, gave the name *drama*, "something done," to their dance-song, and instituted the custom of naming or titling the individual songs. He probably changed the dithyramb from an undisciplined, aimless, partly extemporized song and dance into something of a finished performance. We may, indeed, call him the first "choreographer" of the dithyramb. Arion's dithyramb proved to be a popular success, and it was imitated in many of the other Greek cities. To him was usually given the title of "inventor" of the dithyramb as a poetic and orchestic form.

It is highly probable that when Cleisthenes of Sicyon, at the beginning of the sixth century, transferred the "goat dances" from Adrastus to Dionysus, a competition between groups of performers was instituted. Furthermore, Cleisthenes is believed to have sought the aid of the poet Epigenes in making the songs and dances more attractive.[19] According to one tradition[20] it was in connection with the writings of Epigenes that the saying "[That has] nothing to do with Dionysus" first arose. The expression became proverbial, in the sense of "That has nothing to do with the case." It may indicate that Epigenes actually experimented with the practice, later universally adopted, of setting forth at the Dionysiac festivals the adventures of legendary heroes, as well as those of the god Dionysus.

Later in the sixth century, in the Athenian deme of Icaria, Thespis effected epoch-making changes in the Dionysiac songs and dances of his own community. He is said to have made use of a prologue and of *rhēsis*, "speech," spoken verse. Like Arion, he "poetized" the songs of the chorus, and eliminated improvisation. He acted as *exarchōn* himself. In that capacity, he introduced

---

[19] Flickinger (above, note 1), p. 15.

[20] Suidas and Photius *s.vv.* "Ouden pros ton Dionyson." See Pickard-Cambridge (1st ed.; above, note 1), pp. 166-167; (2nd ed.; above, note 1), pp. 124-126; Gerald F. Else, "The Origin of *Tragoedia*" (above, note 1), p. 45.

[6]

an important innovation: instead of merely displaying virtuosity in song or dance, or merely telling his story in the third person, he assumed the role of a character mentioned in the song—presumably Dionysus himself, or a mythological hero—and, with much dignity, spoke or chanted in alternation with the chorus. In performances of this sort the *exarchōn* came to be called technically an "answerer," *hypokritēs*, because of his relationship to the chorus.[21] Later, of course, *hypokritēs* became the regular Greek word for "actor."

In the year 534, Peisistratus, then "tyrant" or dictator of Athens, established there the great festival of the City Dionysia, in which, amid much splendor and festivity, Dionysus was honored upon the return of spring. An outstanding feature of the celebration was a contest in *tragoedia,* which seems to mean "goat song."[22] Thespis won the first contest, and received the "goat prize." From the *tragoedia* of Thespis Greek tragedy is said to have developed, and Thespis was thereafter regarded as the "father" of Greek drama. The dithyramb, on the other hand, remained a choric song and dance throughout its history.[23]

The Athenian dithyramb developed rapidly, and became a performance of great dignity and beauty. The Dorian Lasus, working at the court of Peisistratus, is said to have been instrumental in bringing it to a high artistic level. Lasus was particularly interested in music. Under his direction the dithyramb continued to use the stirring Phrygian mode, and, in harmony with his music, it

---

[21] Gerald F. Else, in *"Hypokritēs," Wiener Studien,* LXXII (1959), 75-107, contends that the first "actor" was called *tragoidos,* and that the designation *hypokritēs* as a technical term in the theatre dates from about 500 B.C., and denotes the performer customarily called the second actor. Cf. also Else's "The Case of the Third Actor," *Transactions of the American Philological Association* LXXVI, (1945), 1-10; and Pickard-Cambridge (2nd ed., above, note 1), p. 79.

[22] Else and others do not accept this interpretation of the word.

[23] Pickard-Cambridge (1st ed.; above, note 1), pp. 218-220, sees the early performances as of three different types: (1) the dithyramb, which came under the influence of the early Dorian lyric, and became a literary composition; (2) the dances of the satyrs or *sileni,* "which became partly assimilated to tragedy"; and (3) "crude dramatic or semi-dramatic performances" which had no satyr choruses, and which "contained the first elements of solemnity and dealt with death and sorrow," were led by an *exarchōn,* and were "grafted on to" the Dionysia.

[7]

took on a stanzaic or strophic form.[24] We may assume almost with certainty that Lasus also improved and enriched the dance of the dithyramb, for the Greeks customarily regarded song, music, and the dance as forming a single art, which they called *mousikē*. Also, Lasus and his successors seem to have standardized the number of the *choreutae* in a dithyrambic chorus at fifty.

Other famous poets who produced dithyrambs of great majesty and originality were Simonides and Bacchylides of Ceos, and Pindar of Thebes. We have portions of several dithyrambs written by these men. The poems of Bacchylides, as they have come down to us, bear titles—e.g., "Heracles," "The Youths or Theseus," "Io," etc.—indicating mythological but non-Dionysiac themes. They are in balanced strophes, with, in general, smooth, carefully-worked, dignified lyric meters.

In the year 508 B.C. there was established at the City Dionysia a contest in dithyrambic song and dance, as distinct from the now dramatic *tragoedia*. A "foreign" poet, Hypodicus of Chalcis, is recorded as the first victor.

Let us consider now the actual dithyrambic performances of the best period in Athens, as they were set forth in the Dionysiac theatre, in the presence not only of the Athenian populace, but of envoys and visitors who flocked to Athens from all over the Greek world.

We have a fair amount of information about these performances. We know, for example, that at this period there were regularly two dithyrambic contests at the City Dionysia—one for boys and one for men. In each of the two contests five choruses competed, and each chorus consisted of fifty *choreutae*. Thus, in all, five hundred singers and dancers took part annually in the dithyrambic contests of this great festival. Each chorus represented one of the ten tribes of the Athenian people. The *choreutae* were chosen by tribal officials. Scrupulous precautions were taken lest any foreigner, any descendant of a foreigner, anyone suffering under a civil disability, or any person not an actual freeborn blood-member of the tribe for which he danced be included among them. In the rare cases when outsiders did manage to get into the

---

[24] Information on Greek music may be found in such works as Curt Sachs' *The Rise of Music in the Ancient World* (New York, 1943) and F. A. Wright's *The Arts in Greece* (London, 1923), pp. 37-73.

choruses, heavy fines were levied on officials of the tribe concerned.[25]

The singers and dancers were trained with the rigorous care which a religious ritual demanded. Complete responsibility for the training of each chorus rested upon a *chorēgus*—a rich man who had volunteered or who had been designated for this service by the officials of his tribe eleven months before the festival. If the poet was himself to act as leader and trainer of the chorus—a very common procedure—the *chorēgus* cooperated closely with him, and sometimes furnished him an assistant, *hypodidaskalos*. In later days, when the poet no longer participated actively in the training and in the performance, the *chorēgus* chose and hired a *didaskalos*, or instructor, and a *coryphaeus*, or leader of the chorus. The *coryphaeus* served as a sort of concert-master to the *didaskalos*, assisting in arranging the other singers and in rehearsing them. During the singing, it was he who kept the beat, and signaled to the others when to begin, when to step out in the dance, etc. In some cases he may actually have been given a short solo part in the dithyramb.

The poet or, a little later, the *chorēgus*, hired the flute-player—a functionary of great importance, since he was to play all the music for the chorus, and presumably to compose it as well. He would be a highly skilled musician, and would be able to adapt the accepted Phrygian or Hypophrygian mode to the song and to the singers. During the entrance the flute-player regularly walked along with the *choreutae*. During the dancing he seems at times, at least, to have stood in the center of their circle; some writers[26] believe that he stood on the low step which supported the *thymelē*, the altar of Dionysus in the center of the *orchēstra*, or "dancing-place."

The flute-player would, of course, choose a flute of the proper size to harmonize with the voices of his chorus. There were flutes of different sizes for men's and boys' voices, but even so we hear complaints that the sound of the flutes sometimes rose above that of the voices. This is difficult to understand, when we recall that each chorus was composed of fifty voices. It has been suggested

---

[25] Plutarch *Phocion* 30; cf. Demosthenes *Meid.* 56.
[26] A. W. Pickard-Cambridge, *The Theatre of Dionysus at Athens* (Oxford, 1946), pp. 9, 131-132.

[9]

that great accuracy and distinctness of diction was essential, so that the complicated, subtle poetry of the dithyramb might be intelligible to the great audience in the theatre, and that this distinctness may at times have been marred slightly by the flute.

During the period of preparation the *choreutae*, with their instructor and musicians, were sometimes housed with the *choregus*, or at least had their rehearsal room in his home.[27] He seems to have furnished their meals—and the *choreutae* were proverbially hungry.[28] The *choregus* also purchased or rented the costumes which the *choreutae* would wear at the festival. We read of great extravagance on the part of some *choregi*, in their endeavor to present a spectacular effect. In the fourth century, at least, there are reports of *choregi* (among them the orator Demosthenes) who even used gold in the costumes or wreaths of their *choreutae*;[29] however, we are not sure whether the performances concerned were dithyrambic, tragic, or comic. Further, the fabulous nature of the stories is spoiled a little by the fact that in that century the size of all choruses had been considerably reduced. In general, in the classical period the dithyrambic *choreutae* seem to have been dressed in effective but not too sumptuous garments, and to have worn wreaths of fresh flowers and ivy. Apparently they did not wear masks.

There seems to have been intense rivalry among *choregi*, even during the period of rehearsal, and we hear of street fights between adherents of rival *choregi*. Many rich men sought to further their political aspirations by making a good showing in the dithyrambic contests, and it is true that public respect and political preferment did often compensate the *choregus* for his not inconsiderable service to the state. Also, he enjoyed no small distinction during the whole of the time in which he was *choregus*. As a religious official, his person, like that of the *choreutae* and of every other participant in the Dionysia, was sacred throughout his tenure of office, and persons who harmed him, or even touched him, were subject to severe legal penalties for sacrilege and desecration.

It is probable that during the fifth and fourth centuries the

[27] Antiphon *Or.* 6.11-13.
[28] Plutarch *Glor. Ath.* 349 A.
[29] Isocrates *Areop.* 53-54; Athenaeus 3.103 F; Demosthenes *Meid.* 16.

dithyrambic contests were held on the second and third days of the City Dionysia—that is, after the great Dionysiac procession, and before the tragic competition.[30] They were held in the open air, in full daylight, in the *orchēstra* or "dancing-place" of the theatre of Dionysus.

When the opening of the dithyrambic contests had been signaled by a trumpet,[31] and the name of the first tribe had been called by the herald, the dithyrambic *choreutae* of that tribe, wearing their festal garb and wreaths, marched into the *orchēstra* by one of the *parodoi*, or side entrances. They were in single file, in a long line led by their poet or their *coryphaeus*, and followed by their flute-player. They seem at once to have formed a circle around the altar, and to have begun their song. In this formation the *coryphaeus* apparently at times occupied a central position.[32]

We know or can conjecture several things about the choreography of the dithyrambic dance. In the first place, the dithyrambic performances are repeatedly called "thymelic" or "cyclic" by Greek writers. Accordingly we may assume that in the best period, at least, the choreographic pattern of the fifty dancers was circular, around the altar. This pattern puts the dithyramb into the great group of magic encircling dances in which an object is set apart from things of everyday life by the living wall of the dancers' bodies, and is thereby symbolically consecrated, protected, and worshipped. Simple as such a pattern is, it has a religious significance among many peoples.

A scholiast on a passage in the *Hecuba* of Euripides[33] states that on the strophe of a choric ode the *choreutae* "sang while moving to the right," on the antistrophe while moving to the left, and on the epode while standing still. For a long time students of the drama assumed that this statement referred to the chorus of tragedy, since the comment was made directly upon a passage in a tragedy. Some scholars took the statement as implying a march from left to right across the *orchēstra*, then a return in the same

---

[30] A. E. Haigh, *The Attic Theatre* (3rd ed.; Oxford, 1907), p. 24, expressed the belief that they were held on the sixth day, or on the fifth and sixth days; A. W. Pickard-Cambridge, *The Dramatic Festivals at Athens* (Oxford, 1953), p. 64, thought they were held on the first day of the festival.

[31] Pollux 4.88.

[32] Athenaeus 4.152 B.

[33] Schol. *Hecuba* 647, p. 211 Dindorf.

[11]

way from right to left. Others took it as referring to a circular motion around the altar in the *orchēstra,* first to the dancers' right, then to their left. We shall not here enter into the endless controversy on the subject. Suffice it to say that the statement is generally discredited today insofar as tragedy is concerned, but that it is regarded as having some validity for the circular dithyramb.[34] In a cyclic dance, it would be entirely natural for the chorus to circle the altar, moving in one direction on the strophe—to the right, i.e., counterclockwise—then turning the line of direction and circling the altar with a counter-movement on the antistrophe —to the left, i.e., clockwise—and standing still on the epode. It seems likely that this is just what the dithyrambic chorus did. In any case, the balancing rhythms of strophe and antistrophe would indicate balancing patterns of movement.

The commentator on the *Hecuba* does not stop at this point, however. He proceeds to connect the movement which he has described with the heavens, and says that the first part portrays "the movement of the heavens from east to west," the second part the "movement of the planets" from west to east, and the third, with the *choreutae* singing while standing still, the stationary position of the earth. In these words he evidently places the dance of which he is speaking among what are known as cosmic dances—those in which the movements of the heavenly bodies are portrayed or symbolized.

There is some evidence tending to support the theory of a cosmic element in the dance of the dithyramb.[35] A fragment of Ptolemaeus, for example, says that the cyclic choruses portray "the movement of the sun." Also, there were cosmic dances in antiquity, among many peoples,[36] and the Greeks themselves believed that the movements of the heavenly bodies in themselves constituted a cosmic dance.[37] However, since a cosmic dance seems irrelevant

---

[34] A. E. Haigh (above, note 30), pp. 315-316.

[35] *Et. Mag.* 690.50-57, *s.v.* "prosōdion"; cf. Sophocles *Antigone* 1146 and schol. ad loc.; Menander Rhet. 9.329; Lillian B. Lawler, "Cosmic Dance and Dithyramb," *Studies in Honor of Ullman* (St. Louis, 1960), pp. 12-16.

[36] Fritz Weege, *Der Tanz in der Antike* (Halle/Saale, 1926), p.19; W. O. E. Oesterley, *The Sacred Dance* (New York, 1923), pp. 69-72, 95-96; Cook (above, note 15), I, 472-495; cf. J. G. Frazer, *The Golden Bough* (New York, 1951), VI, 142; VII, 311.

[37] Lucian *Salt.* 7; Euripides *Electra* 464-468; *Ion* 1078-1080; Philo *On*

to the cult of Dionysus,[38] it is possible that any such pattern in the dithyramb was probably not native to that dance, but may have been borrowed and absorbed into it from other dances. Like many other aspects of a culture, dances are often the product of a fusion of originally discrete elements.

Much of the dancing to the dithyramb, as to any Greek choral song, would not be seem to be dancing at all in the eyes of a modern observer. The dance, naturally, had begun as rhythmical movements of the feet and legs,[39] but had been considerably extended in scope until it was regarded as including rhythmical movements of any sort, including the highly conventionalized gestures known collectively as *cheironomia*. One could "dance" the meaning of a song with rhythmical movements of the body or limbs, or with mimetic or symbolic gestures and postures, and one could accompany the spoken word similarly with explanatory gestures.[40] The Greeks greatly admired the art of *cheironomia;* in matters of aesthetics their taste is usually above reproach, and we may credit their judgment in this matter without hesitation. Unfortunately, we know all too little about the developed *cheironomia*. In general effect it must have been something like the code of stylized gestures, *hastas* and *mudras,* which can still be seen in the old rituals and dances of India.[41] We are informed that lengthy stories could be "told" in the dance by means of gestures, and that even foreigners could follow their meaning. The expressive "dancing" of choral songs by the Greeks seems to have reached its greatest height during the fifth century; for shortly afterwards we find a poet complaining[42] that the *choreutae* of his day, in contrast to the fine dancers of former times, merely stand and howl, and "do nothing"—as if they had suffered a paralytic stroke!

The ordinary cyclic performance of the best period may in

Creation 23.70; cf. Aristotle *Meteor.* 1.343 B, 23, where a comet's progress is called a great leap, *halma,* a technical term in the dance.

[38] Lewis R. Farnell, *Cults of the Greek States* (Oxford, 1896-1909), V, 99-101.

[39] Athenaeus 14.630 C.

[40] Athenaeus 1.21 F-22 A; 14.628 D-E; Aristotle *Poetics* 1461 B, 26, to 1462 A, 10; Lucian *Salt.* 63; cf. Plato *Rep.* 3.396 A-B; *Laws* 7.816 A.

[41] R. M. Hughes, *The Gesture Language of the Hindu Dance* (New York, 1941); P. S. Naidu, "Hastas," *New Indian Antiquary,* 1 (1938), 345-361.

[42] Athenaeus 14.628 E.

general have taken some such form as this: the march into the *orchēstra;* a strophe, sung with *counterclockwise* walking in a circle, and accompanying gestures; an antistrophe sung with *clockwise* walking in a circle, and accompanying gestures; then perhaps an epode, sung in a standing position, again with appropriate gestures; a repetition of this pattern until the song was ended; then a graceful and stately circle dance, to the same melody as that of the song; and finally the march out, in a line, with the flute-player bringing up the rear.

After all the tribal groups had completed their performances, the judges voted, and a herald then announced the winning tribe in the boys' division and that in the men's division. The *chorēgus* and the poet of each victorious chorus, in festal garb, came forward and received the plaudits of the crowd, and were then crowned with ivy and flowers. To each winning *chorēgus,* not as an individual but as representative of his tribe, was given a fine bronze tripod—after the manner of our loving cups or trophies. Prizes of some sort or other seem to have been given also to the victorious poets, at least up to about 501 B.C., when the festival of the City Dionysia was reorganized. There is some evidence that the two winning poets may have been taken to their homes in chariots, with a cheering crowd following along with each.[43]

After the festival was over, the winning poets and *chorēgi* customarily made a sacrifice to Dionysus, and then joined with their *choreutae,* instructors, musicians, and friends, in a feast. Sometimes an overjoyed *chorēgus* even gave wine to the populace, in celebration of his triumph. Shortly afterwards, the two winning *chorēgi* dedicated their tripods to the god, setting them up, at their own expense, in a public place, on artistically designed bases, inscribed with the record of the victory.

In spite of the generally staid and conventional nature of the dithyrambic performances in the fifth century, there is some evidence that even in the first half of that century poets were thinking in terms of newer and freer forms. The great Theban poet Pindar, for example, was evidently not satisfied with the usual themes and motifs, superbly as he could handle them. In some of his experiments in theme, versification, dance, and music—the

---

[43] Pickard-Cambridge (1st ed.; above, note 1), p. 52.

"audacis . . . dithyrambos" attributed to him by Horace (*Carm.* 4. 2. 10)—he foreshadowed the less austere dithyramb which was to become popular after his death. A significant example is furnished by his dithyramb entitled "Heracles the Bold, or Cerberus, for the Thebans,"[44] some thirty lines of which, altogether, have been preserved, in fragments. In this poem many of the readings are uncertain, and there have been varying restorations of the text; but Pindar seems to say that "new gates have been opened for the [sacred] cyclic choruses." He apparently says also that in former days the dithyramb "crawled [as a serpent], dragging a rope" *(heirpe schoinoteneia t' aoida dithyrambōn).* The adjective is usually interpreted as "long-drawn out" (cf. Hermogenes *De Invent.* 4.3); however, it may possibly refer to an occasional use in the early dithyramb of a "rope-carrying" or "crossed hands" alignment of the performers (see below, pp. 83-85). Pindar proceeds to a vivid description of an orgiastic dance like that of Maenads and satyrs in frenzied Dionysiac rites—a dance here said to be performed by various Greek divinities in honor of Dionysus on his festal day, in the presence of the Mother of the Gods, the great nature divinity of Asia Minor. The musical instruments accompanying this wild dance are *tympana* or hand-drums, and *krotala* or castanets—both commonly used in orgiastic rituals to increase the frenzy of dancers and spectators. The divine dancers toss their heads and shout unrestrainedly. Zeus himself shakes his thunderbolt (as Maenads and satyrs are said to shake their *thyrsi*), and the snakes on the aegis of Athena hiss (as do the snakes carried by these same Dionysiac dancers). There is also a reference to Artemis, who has "yoked wild lions" for the ritual, and who "rejoices, too, in dancing herds of animals." The whole, with its overtones of savagery and its hint of a return to primitive ritual, raises interesting questions as to how this particular dithyramb of Pindar's was actually performed with song and dance—if it ever was so performed. There is no record in extant Greek literature of any actual performances that experimented with "orgiastic" dithyrambic dances in Pindar's day.

There was experimentation of other sorts, however. Early in the fifth century, flute-players were introducing into the dithy-

---

[44] Fragment 70 b, Snell.

rambs certain musical innovations which many poets decried as attempts to render the music supreme over the song and dance. Pratinas, who wrote both dithyrambs and tragedies, and who was noted particularly for the prominent part which the dance played in his performances, attacked vehemently the new style of music in a passage which has come down to us.[45] Experimentation reached its height in the late fifth and the early fourth century, in what is called the "new dithyramb." Apparently feeling ran high in Athens over the relative merits of the new and the old cyclic choruses. Aristophanes assailed the innovations with vigor (cf. *Clouds* 970-972). The populace seems in general to have liked the new forms—although there is a record of an audience hissing a performance of Timotheus.[46] An unknown comic poet, reputedly Pherecrates, in his play *Cheiron*[47] personifies Mousikē, and portrays her as complaining bitterly and at length of the "mutilations" she has received at the hands of various "new" poets and musicians. She speaks particularly of one of the dithyrambic poets, Cinesias, calling him "accursed" and deploring the "inharmonious twists" of his music and poetry.

In general, the new cyclic performance was a reaction from the dignified, elevated dithyramb of the middle of the fifth century. It was unconventional, less austere, more emotional, even a little sensational. Some of the new poets must have been sincere, and genuinely convinced of the need for less restraint in the genre. However, as is often the case, many men of limited talent, impatient with time-honored canons which were difficult to observe, plunged wholeheartedly into the new movement in dithyrambic composition and performance, and evidently went to extremes in it. They seem to have endeavored to substitute freakishness for the genius which they lacked.

---

[45] Athenaeus 14.617 B-F. Ervin Roos, in *Die tragische Orchestik im Zerrbild der altattischen Komödie* (Lund, 1961), believes that the ode is from a satyr play, is sung by satyrs playing *citharae* and attacking flute music, and does not reflect the views of Pratinas himself. Webster (Pickard-Cambridge, 2nd ed.; above, note 1, p 20) thinks that it may be from a dithyramb sung by men costumed as satyrs.

[46] Plutarch *An sit seni* 795 D. Timotheus produced one dithyramb entitled "The Birth-Pangs of Semele," which is said to have been very "noisy"! Cf. Athenaeus 8.352 A.

[47] Fragment 145 K, ap. Pseudo-Plutarch *De musica* 30.1141 D-F, 1142 A.

Characteristic of the new dithyramb, we are told, was a greater emphasis upon music and upon versatility on the part of the musicians. In fact, in many cases the music seems to have been treated as of more importance than the words of the song. No longer was it a simple air in the Phrygian mode, performed on the double flute. In the hands of Timotheus and his followers, the music of the dithyramb became soft, flexible, and varied. In structure it was highly elaborate, with many "twists and turns," flourishes, runs, and trills, and with a mixture of modes and styles which to the conservative Greek of the day must have seemed indeed "corrupted," "weak," and "effeminate." (Cf. Plato *Laws* 3.700 D.) In contrast to the older music, in which there was a separate note for each syllable of the song, the new music sometimes allowed several notes to one syllable. Apparently the *cithara*, or lyre, and other instruments were used instead of, or more probably as a supplement to, the flute. The stanzaic form of the song, with balanced strophes and antistrophes, was in general abandoned.[48] Solos *(anabolai)* were introduced, accompanied in some cases by the lyre—in other words, lyric interludes. There is even a possibility that recitatives, to a background of music, were used from time to time.

There is evidence that the poets of the new dithyrambs affected elaborate figures of speech, long, bombastic, high-flown words, some of them of their own coinage, and perhaps even combinations of unintelligible syllables designed to give special effects. Aristophanes travesties all these tendencies mercilessly.[49]

The new poets made changes also in methods of production. In many cases the poet no longer served as chorus leader. Even if he did not, however, he sometimes entered with his chorus, to speak or sing a prologue *(prooimion, anabolē, eisbolē)*, often long-winded and rambling, setting forth the story to be told in the dithyramb.[50] Then the poet retired, and the singing and dancing of the dithyramb proper began. At the end of the performance he sometimes returned to deliver an epilogue *(epilogos)*, which, we are told, usually contained a prayer.

The performances of the new dithyrambs are said to have been

---

48 Aristotle *Probl.* 19.15.918 B, 18-20.
49 Cf. *Birds* 1372-1409; *Frogs* 209-269 and 1286-1296.
50 Cf. Aristotle *Rhet.* 3.8.9.1409 A; cf. schol. Aristophanes *Clouds* 596.

far more "mimetic" than were their predecessors.[51] This statement implies a greater use in them of dancing and gesture. On some occasions the *choreutae* must have been called upon to express mimetically certain concepts very difficult to portray. In this connection the choregic monument of Lysicrates in Athens, celebrating a dithyrambic victory of 335/4 B.C., is of great interest. The frieze of the monument depicts what seems to have been the theme of the winning dithyramb—the story of the Tyrrhenian pirates who were changed into dolphins by Dionysus; figures with human bodies, dolphins' heads, and no arms, are portrayed as leaping into the sea. Some writers[52] have seen in them actual dithyrambic *choreutae*, enacting the story! It appears more likely that the reliefs are purely mythological. In the dithyramb itself, any suggestion of the transformation of the men into dolphins must have come from highly stylized gestures and dance movements on the part of the *choreutae*. Any descent into the ludicrous would of necessity be banned with rigor from a ceremonial dithyramb— even a new dithyramb!

Ancient writers mention a great many of the new dithyrambists. For our purposes it will suffice to consider in detail one only, Cinesias,[53] whom we have already mentioned, for we have more information about his dances than about those of any other poet of his group.

Cinesias lived in the late fifth and early fourth century. His father and grandfather were *citharoedi*, and Cinesias seems to have inherited from them some inclination toward music, song, and the dance, with a special leaning to the dithyramb. Aligning himself with the new movement, he seems to have bent his efforts to delighting the rabble rather than to improving his art. To Aristophanes, both Platos, and Plutarch, he was an unspeakably bad dithyrambist. He is said also to have been a man of low moral character. He apparently suffered from tuberculosis, and was weak, sallow, emaciated, and unsteady on his legs.

---

[51] Aristotle (above, note 48).

[52] Cf. Maurice Emmanuel, *Essai sur l'Orchestique Grecque* (Paris, 1895), pp. 259-260.

[53] Lillian B. Lawler, " 'Limewood' Cinesias and the Dithyrambic Dance," *Transactions of the American Philological Association*, LXXXI (1950), 78-88.

[18]

We are told[54] that Cinesias devised and taught the dances with which the members of the chorus accompanied his verses. Such "dances," of course, would include steps, gestures, and choreography.

The scene in the *Birds* of Aristophanes (1372-1409) in which he is ridiculed is very interesting. It abounds in references to flying, and shows what we, too, would call the "high-flown" style of the new dithyramb. Also, the lines give opportunity for extravagant "flying" gestures as the scene is performed—a fact which may point to excessive arm-flapping in Cinesias' dances.

A passage in the *Frogs* (146-153) is pertinent in this connection. There Heracles, preparing Dionysus for his visit to the realm of the dead, tells him of a great slough, in which languish criminals of many sorts. Among them, says Heracles, would be such a man as would "copy out a speech from Morsimus," one of the lesser lights among the writers of tragedy. Dionysus, improving upon his jest, adds also, "whoever has learned the pyrrhic dance of Cinesias."[55] Many interpretations of this passage have been suggested: that Cinesias actually arranged a pyrrhic dance; that he inserted a real pyrrhic dance into one of his dithyrambs; that his dances were full of lively movement; that he gestured violently, as if fighting an enemy, when he recited his own lines; that he used for his cyclic choruses music written for the pyrrhic dance. The pyrrhic at this time was an idealized "war" dance. Plato (*Laws* 7.815 A-B) gives a good description of it: it makes use, he says, of movements used by soldiers in avoiding missiles of various sorts, in throwing weapons, in shooting arrows, in striking blows with and without arms. Surely the comic poet's point in calling Cinesias' dance a pyrrhic is that his dance is frequently too brisk, too active, too full of sharp, even contorted, gestures and postures to be appropriate for the dithyramb. Violent and contorted movements in the dance were regarded as "ignoble" or "wicked" (*phaulai*).[56]

The choreography of Cinesias' dances, also, must have been

---

54 Aristophanes *Frogs* 153 and schol. ad loc.; *Birds* 1403-1404 and schol. ad loc.; Suidas *s.v.* "Pyrrhichais."

55 *Frogs* 153; cf. schol. ad loc.

56 Plato *Laws* 2.670 D; 7.798 D-816 E; Athenaeus 14.628 D-629 B; Pseudo-Plutarch *De musica* 1131-1147, *passim*.

startlingly unusual and varied, if we can judge by comments upon them. Writers speak of his "twists and turns, lacking all harmony," and frequently use the verb *kamptō*, "twist, turn," or its derivatives, in referring to his dances.[57] In general, the movement of his cyclic chorus must still have been in a circle, but it must have been varied freely, so as to permit the individual dancers to move about with some independence, rather than as one harmonious whole. Perhaps the movement of the dancers, instead of being a straightforward walk, may have shown variations—abrupt reversals of direction, for instance, or individual circling, or a break-up of the chorus into smaller groups with varying patterns of movement—or even some "hesitation" or breaking of the rhythm; the word *oknēros*, "hesitant," is one of the adjectives applied to Cinesias.[58]

There has been much speculation as to whether Cinesias did or did not take part in public performances of his dithyrambs. If he was as weak as the ancient writers indicate, he probably did not actually dance with his chorus; he may have appeared in his prologues, and "danced" to them by means of symbolic gestures and postures.

The sum-total of the evidence from Greek writers would seem to be, in effect, that the weak-legged Cinesias, indecent in his personal life and audacious in his handling of the sacred dithyramb, had cheapened the cyclic chorus with his new-fangled figures and gestures, which were not only undignified, unrestrained, and inappropriate, but often even wanton. "Why do you come here," says Aristophanes, through the mouth of his protagonist (*Birds* 1378), to Cinesias, "shaking your wobbly foot around and around in your twisted, crooked cyclic dance?" It is interesting to note that sometimes *kyllos*, "crooked," has the same double meaning as has its English equivalent!

Dithyrambic choruses were very popular in Athens and in other cities as well. As early as the fifth century, they had begun to transcend the bounds of the City Dionysia. In time they were featured on various other important occasions—at other Dionysiac festivals, and also at the Prometheia, the Poseidonia, the Hephaes-

---

[57] Pseudo-Plutarch *De musica* 1141 E, line 14; cf. Aristophanes *Clouds* 333 and schol. ad loc.; 970-971.

[58] Schol. *Frogs* 153; Suidas *s.v.* "Pyrrhichais."

teia, and the Panathenaea. A fifth-century red-figured bell krater in the Metropolitan Museum of Art in New York,[59] attributed to Polion, shows three dancing satyrs wearing fleecy white garments. An inscription on the jar attests the fact that they were performers at the Panathenaea; they are believed to represent participants in a dithyramb.

Dithyrambs came to be used frequently in the worship of Apollo, in Athens and elsewhere. They are attested at the Thargelia in Athens, at the Pythia and Soteria in Delphi, at the Apollonia on the island of Delos. Also, they became a favored means of honoring and invoking the healing god Asclepius, "son of Apollo." The magnificent theatre in which dithyrambs were sung in the worship of Asclepius still survives at Epidaurus, the chief center of his cult.

The dithyramb continues on in Athens for many centuries, changing constantly. The number of *choreutae* in a dithyrambic chorus dwindles from fifty, and we hear of thirty-five, twenty-five, fifteen, twelve, seven, five, and even as few as three. There is an increasing emphasis on showy solos and on elaborate music, until the dithyramb stands almost on the threshold of professionalism. As the cost of producing the performances becomes a burden, various steps are taken to relieve the financial pressure. A city official, the *agōnothetēs*, takes over the functions of the *chorēgus*. Sometimes two men act as joint *chorēgī* for a performance, or two or more tribes may cooperate on one chorus. Finally, in the second century of our era, all the tribes unite in a single performance.

The dithyrambic competition seems to have ended at that time. Thenceforth, cyclic performances appear to have been produced without rivalry, and indeed many old dithyrambs of high literary merit were revived. The exact date of the termination of the dithyrambic performances is unknown.

---

[59] No. 25.78.66. See Gisela M. A. Richter, *Attic Red-Figured Vases—A Survey* (New Haven, 1946), p. 145.

[21]

II | THE DANCE
OF TRAGEDY

In the previous chapter, we have seen that, from primitive performances, two poetic genres had evolved—dithyramb and *tragoedia*. The latter developed rapidly, and became Greek tragedy.[1]

In the best period of the Greek drama, the chorus always formed an integral and vital part of a tragedy; in fact, a tragedy as presented in a Greek theatre must have resembled an impressive semi-operatic spectacle rather than a drama, as we use the word today.

The Greek tragic poets were fully aware of the importance of the dance in their productions. The early playwrights Thespis, Pratinas, and Phrynichus were actually called "dancers"; and Phrynichus boasted that he had made use of as many dance figures as there were "waves in a stormy sea."[2] Like Phrynichus, Aeschylus instructed his own choruses in dancing, and invented figures, *schēmata*, for them. Euripides also seems to have been much interested in the dance, for his plays are exceptionally rich in incidental dances of many types. Sophocles, trained in music and dancing from childhood, played the lyre in one of his own plays *(Thamyris)* and performed with marked grace a ball-playing dance in another *(Nausicaä)*.[3] Sophocles even composed a prose work on the tragic chorus and its dance. Unfortunately this book has not come down to us. However, we have a great deal of

---

[1] For works on the origin of the Greek drama in general and of tragedy see note 1 of the preceding chapter.

[2] Plutarch *Quaest. conv.* 8.9.3.732 F.

[3] Athenaeus 1.20 F; 21 E-F; 22 A.

information on the dance of tragedy, from scattered references in the works of various Greek writers, and from comments in the text of the extant plays themselves.

The lexicographer Pollux (4.110) says that originally, and up to the time of Aeschylus, the tragic chorus consisted of fifty singers and dancers, *choreutae*. Some scholars have challenged this statement.[4] Certainly in the fifth century the number was fifteen—at which number it remained until the end of the classical period. In the post-classical period there may have been at times as few as seven.[5] There was always a *coryphaeus*, or leader of the chorus, as there was in the dithyrambic performance. It is believed that some of the lines assigned to the chorus were sung, some were delivered in recitative, and some were spoken, usually by the *coryphaeus*.

Like the actors, members of the chorus were always men; they frequently impersonated women. They wore masks. Their costumes were considerably less elaborate than were those of the actors—closer to the dress of everyday life and suitable to the group of persons whom the chorus portrayed in the play, but still more ornate than ordinary clothing. Their shoes were probably low and soft, to facilitate movement in the dance; from the time of Sophocles on, these shoes are said to have been white. The *choreutae* often wore cloaks; presumably, as in comedy,[6] they may sometimes have laid these aside before engaging in a dance or other activity. Often the members of the chorus carried the tall walking-sticks so favored by Athenian citizens. The flute-player, who walked along with the chorus, wore a long, rich, figured garment.[7]

As in the case of the chorus of the dithyramb, the cost of the costumes for the tragic chorus, or their rental, and the expenses involved in the training of the chorus, were borne by a *chorēgus*.

---

[4] Cf. A. W. Pickard-Cambridge, *Dithyramb, Tragedy, and Comedy* (1st ed.; Oxford, 1927), pp. 87-89.

[5] A wall painting (no longer extant), found in a grave of the Roman imperial period in Cyrene, showed three tragic actors and a chorus of seven young men, wearing wreaths. See A. W. Pickard-Cambridge, *The Dramatic Festivals of Athens* (Oxford, 1953), Fig. 120, between pp. 232 and 233.

[6] Aristophanes *Acharn.* 627; *Peace* 729; *Thesmo.* 656; *Lys.* 637, 662-663, 685-686; cf. Athenaeus 10.417 F.

[7] For the masks, costumes, and footwear of tragic actors and *choreutae*, see Pickard-Cambridge, *Dramatic Festivals* (above, note 5), pp. 175-238.

[23]

However, in the event of a victory in competition, the dramatic *choregus* received no reward beyond a crown of ivy—and, of course, great glory. In addition to a similar crown, the winning poet was in early times given a goat, in classical times probably a money award.

Like the dance of the dithyramb, the dance of tragedy in the classical period was accompanied by the music of the double flute or, occasionally, of the *cithara* or hand-harp. Later both instruments were used. In a passage in which he makes fun of Euripides' choral odes, Aristophanes (*Frogs* 1304-1307) calls for castanets *(ostraka)* as an appropriate accompaniment to them; however the scene is a burlesque, and we probably need not take the suggestion too seriously.

There was no harmony or counterpoint, as we know it, in the music of the Greeks, and both instrument and voice followed the melody.[8] Various genres of flute music were recognized,[9] among which one in particular, the piercing *gingras*, seems to have been particularly suited to the laments of tragedy. We shall consider others later. Greek music also made use of "modes," which may have corresponded roughly to what we know as "keys," but which had in addition certain emotional associations. The stately Dorian mode, the more impassioned Phrygian mode, the sad Lydian and Mixolydian modes, the dignified Ionian mode, were all used effectively in connection with tragedy. In the late fifth and the fourth century Greek music underwent a tremendous change; the old distinctions between the modes were almost broken down, and musicians vied with one another in spectacular trills, flourishes, and *tours de force* of all kinds. Euripides and contemporary writers of tragedy were influenced by the new music, but perhaps less so than were the dithyrambic poets. Euripides' use of innovations in music and in rhythm is burlesqued heartily in Aristophanes' *Frogs* (1309-1322), and the florid character of his trills is indicated by such freak words as *eieieieieieilissete* (1314). On a small piece of papyrus found in comparatively recent times, we actually have a few lines (338-343) from the *parodos* of the

---

[8] For general information on Greek music see Curt Sachs, *The Rise of Music in the Ancient World* (New York, 1943); also F. A. Wright, *The Arts in Greece* (London, 1923), pp. 37-73.

[9] Athenaeus 14.618 C; 4.174 F-175 A-B.

Orestes of Euripides, with symbols indicating musical notes written above them.[10] However, the papyrus was written some four hundred years after the death of Euripides; also, it is very fragmentary, and its interpretation is extremely uncertain.

The accompanist in Greek tragedy was a person of great consequence; he was indeed both composer and performer. Originally hired by the tragic poet himself, and subject to his close supervision, the flute-player in the fifth century came to be employed by the *chorēgus*, and forthwith embarked upon a course of individuality and virtuosity which sometimes aroused the ire of the poet. The surprisingly violent outburst of Pratinas against this situation, as preserved in Athenaeus (14.617 B-F), refers probably to the dithyramb rather than to tragedy (see above, p. 16), but the poet undoubtedly felt just as strongly with regard to "non-conformity" on the part of accompanists in tragic performances, since he wrote in both genres.

We are told by many writers[11] that the characteristic dance of tragedy was known as *emmeleia,* and that it was a dignified, "noble," or "serious" *(spoudaia)* dance, carefully adjusted to the mood of the lines of the play. Significant in it was *cheironomia,* the code of symbolical gestures. Telestes, one of the dancers or dancing teachers associated with Aeschylus, is said to have been able to portray clearly the whole story of the *Seven against Thebes* by dancing and gesture, without a word.[12] The *choreutae* made use of *cheironomia* not only to accompany their own songs, but also to accompany long speeches of the actors. The actors, too, used stylized gestures.[13] In particular, the actor who as a "messenger" had the difficult task of recounting stirring events

---

[10] The papyrus is now in Vienna, No. 8029 in the Rainer Collection.

[11] Pollux 4.99; Lucian *Salt.* 26; Athenaeus 1.20 E; 14.631 E; Suidas and Hesychius *s.v.* "emmeleia"; cf. Plato *Laws* 7.816 B, C; schol. Aristophanes *Clouds* 540.

[12] Athenaeus 1.21 F, 22 A; cf. a similar feat in much later times, as recorded in Lucian *Salt.* 63.

[13] Athenaeus 1.21 F, 22 A; schol. Aristophanes *Clouds* 1352; Suidas *s.v.* "emmeleia"; cf. Plato *Laws* 7.816 A; *Rep.* 3.396 A-397 B. See also Pickard-Cambridge, *Dramatic Festivals* (above, note 5), pp. 169-174; Anna Spitzbarth, *Untersuchungen zur Spieltechnik der griechischen Tragödie* (Zürich, 1946), *passim;* H. L. Tracy, "Double Tableaux in Greek Tragedy," *Classical Journal* LIII (1958), 338-345; Karl Sittl, *Die Gebärden der Griechen und Römer* (Leipzig, 1890), pp. 199-211; Peter D. Arnott, *An Introduction to the Greek Theatre* (London, 1959), pp. 8-9.

which were presumed to have happened off-scene must have used *cheironomia* constantly. The messengers' speeches of Greek tragedy, accompanied with much gesture, were great favorites of the Greeks. When well done, they held the audience spellbound. There is actually attested a messenger's dance *(angelikē orchēsis, angelikon)*,[14] which "imitated the *schēmata* of messengers," but we have no evidence that it was ever used in tragedy. By the time of Aristotle some of the popular actors used the gestures and *schēmata* of dancing to such an exaggerated extent in accompanying their words that they incurred much criticism.[15] Similar exaggeration in the use of dance-like gestures and postures is ascribed to persons reciting epic or lyric poems in competitions, and even to some flute-players.[16]

We are informed that the chorus of tragedy was essentially a solid rectangle in arrangement and movement,[17] its evolutions suggesting marching rather than dancing. However, as we shall see, there must have been a great deal of freedom for the choreographer within the framework of the play, and striking dances of many sorts seem to have been introduced, if they fitted naturally into the plot.

In some tragedies (cf. the *Suppliants* and *Persians* of Aeschylus) the chorus entered the *orchēstra* at the beginning of the play. In others, the entrance of the chorus, or *parodos*, was prefaced by a prologue, which could be either a monologue or a dialogue. The chorus, with its flute-player, came in from the right of the audience, usually in a rank-and-file alignment of three by five persons when it consisted of fifteen. The ranks were known as *zyga*, the files as *stoichoi*. Entry "by ranks" implied a formation with five persons across the front, and a rectangle three persons deep. Entry "by files" implied three persons across the front, and a rectangle five persons deep.[18] This formal marching entry was customarily accompanied by singing or chanting, and was often in the anapaestic or "marching" meter.

---

[14] Pollux 4.103; Lillian B. Lawler, "The Messenger's Dance," *Classical Outlook*, XXII (1945), 59-61; Gerald F. Else, *"Hypokritēs,"* Wiener Studien LXXII, (1959), 106-107.

[15] Aristotle *Poetics* 1461 B; 1462 A, 1-18.

[16] Aristotle *Poetics* 1461 B, 30-33; 1462 A, 4-8.

[17] *Et. Mag. s.v.* "tragoedia," 764, 5.

[18] Pollux 4.108-109.

In all periods there could be variations in the entrance, to meet the exigencies of the plot. Members of the chorus might enter individually, as, for instance, in the *Trojan Women* of Euripides. Or the entrance might be in the nature of a rout—as perhaps in the *Seven against Thebes* of Aeschylus (at line 78), where the members of the chorus rush in terrified. On occasion the chorus apparently enters quietly, without song or dance, as in the *Orestes* of Euripides, where the *choreutae* are specifically enjoined to silence (136-139; cf. also 140-151) so as not to waken Orestes. Sometimes, in special cases—e.g., in the *Eumenides* of Aeschylus and the *Suppliants* of Euripides—there is no entrance song at all, and the chorus is "discovered" at the beginning of the play. Scholars are not agreed as to how the *choreutae* got into the *orchēstra* under these circumstances, since there was no curtain or similar device to conceal the setting from the audience before the play began; perhaps they merely walked in unobtrusively and took their places in full view of the spectators, before the opening of the play. In any case, in plays of this sort the first song of the chorus after the play began was given the technical name of the *parodos*.

Arrived in the *orchēstra*, the chorus customarily turned and faced the audience. This movement placed the *choreutae* of the left-hand entering rank or file in the front row; accordingly the *coryphaeus* and the best and most attractive-looking singers and dancers were placed in that rank or file, with the *coryphaeus* in the middle. These *choreutae* were called the "standers on the left" (*aristerostatai*), or "first-standers" (*prōtostatai*). The *choreutae* in the middle row or rows were called "second-standers" (*deuterostatai*) or "standers in the alley" (*laurostatai*), and those in the inside row the "right-standers" (*dexiostatai*) or "third-standers" (*tritostatai*). The middle row or rows formed the least honorable position. The last person in each line was called "last man" (*eschatos*) or "the exposed one" (*psileus*) or "border-man" (*kraspeditēs*).[19] It is interesting to note that the technical terms for the various positions in the chorus were the same as those used in military tactics.

A fragment of Menander (153 Koerte, 165 Kock), the comic

---

[19] Pollux 4.106; Hesychius *s.vv.* "psileis," "laurostatai," "aristerostatēs."

poet of the fourth-third century B.C., is of significance here. "Just as in the choruses," he says, "not all the members sing, but two or three stand by silent *(aphōnoi)*, last of all, just to make up the number. . . . They fill up space but there is no real life in them." Menander's reference is probably not to comedy, since the comedy of his day usually did not have a formal integrated chorus. Scholars think the reference may be rather to the chorus of tragedy—particularly as he uses the technical term *eschatoi* of the mute *choreutae.*

The chorus continued to sing and use gestures until the end of the *parodos*. After the *parodos* there ensued a dramatic episode, during which the chorus reacted visibly to the words of the actors, with appropriate grouping, movements, and gestures.[20] Usually the chorus was sympathetic to one or more of the characters in the play, hostile to others, and it showed its feelings in words, actions, and gestures[21]—which latter, as we have noted, were regarded as a form of dancing.

After each episode, the actors apparently withdrew, and the chorus, in song and dance or gesture, expressed further response to what they had said, or, sometimes, relieved the emotional tension of the plot by singing lyrics of mythological or religious inspiration. Such an interlude, called a choral ode or *stasimon,* is frequently divided into strophe, antistrophe, and, sometimes, epode. Often there are three, four, or more balancing strophes and antistrophes, followed by one epode; sometimes there is no epode at all; sometimes there is, instead a *pro-odos,* before the first strophe.

In the previous chapter we observed that various early conjectures to the effect that on the strophe the tragic chorus moved or circled the altar in one direction, on the antistrophe moved back in the opposite direction, and on the epode stood still, have been generally discredited by modern scholarship. Similarly, the attempt to interpret the *stasimon* as a choral passage sung standing, and not accompanied by dancing, since the root *sta-* denotes

---

[20] Schol. Aristophanes *Clouds* 1352; cf. Tracy (above, note 13).
[21] Cf. Famee L. Shisler, "The Use of Stage Business to Portray Emotion in Greek Tragedy," *American Journal of Philology,* LXVI (1945), 377-397; also, "The Technique of the Portrayal of Joy in Greek Tragedy," *Transactions of the American Philological Association,* LXXIII (1942), 277-292.

standing, or causing to stand,[22] has likewise been discredited, chiefly because of certain specific references to dancing in some of the *stasima* themselves,[23] and much evidence for the use of gesture-dancing with the choral songs. The word *stasimon* is now variously explained as denoting (1) an ode sung while the chorus is in the *orchēstra*, not entering or leaving it; or (2) an ode sung by a chorus "set up" or arranged appropriately for the delivery of the ode; or (3) "regular, steady" singing, uninterrupted by dialogue.

The choral odes, to be sung to the music of the flute, are composed in free, varied, complex meters. A close study of the meters may often shed some light on the dance which accompanies them. It is easy to sense mood and tempo, of course, from the content of the verse and from the meter, and frequently the balance of strophe and antistrophe furnishes some clue to choreography; but the complexity of the metrical structure in most cases thwarts any attempt to plot from it precise movements or choreography. In 1871 Hermann Buchholtz published a delightful little volume in which he scrutinized choral meters and indications of movement in the plays of Euripides, to gain some idea of the tragic dance in general.[24] Similarly, in 1898 Christian Kirchhoff attempted to restore the entire dance of Greek tragedy from a painstaking analysis of the meters of the *Hippolytus* of Euripides.[25] However, scholars have tacitly and regretfully agreed that the findings of both these writers were purely conjectural.

Editors and commentators on Greek tragedy occasionally make suggestions as to dance movements appropriate to the meters of the various odes. H. D. F. Kitto has shown particular interest in speculations of this sort.[26] He has noted the "grave, religious, hypnotic effect" of cretic rhythms, the "excited" nature of the dochmiacs, the steady march of the "four-square anapaests," the run-

---

[22] Cf. schol. Euripides *Phoen.* 202; Suidas *s.v.* "stasimon"; schol. Sophocles *Trach.* 216; *Et. Mag.* 690.47-49, *s.v.* "prosōdion."

[23] Cf. Aeschylus *Eumen.* 307; Euripides *Herc. Fur.* 761.

[24] Hermann Buchholtz, *Die Tanzkunst des Euripides* (Leipzig, 1871).

[25] Christian Kirchhoff, *Dramatische Orchestik der Hellenen* (Leipzig, 1898).

[26] H. D. F. Kitto, "The Dance in Greek Tragedy," *Journal of Hellenic Studies* LXXV (1955), 36-41; cf. also his *Greek Tragedy—A Literary Study* (New York, 1961), *passim.*

ning style of the trochees, the strength and stateliness of the dac-
tyls, the smoothness and languor of the ionic *a minore,* with its
"delicious side-step in the middle." He has pointed out also that in
the *Agamemnon,* beginning with the *parodos,* Aeschylus has done
a most unusual thing: He has composed several odes in the same
basic rhythm, the iambic. In fact, from line 192 on, seventeen out
of twenty-one consecutive choral stanzas are written "wholly or
in part in one rhythm." Kitto believes that this circumstance points
to a prolonged sustaining of one dance movement, which is here
designed to give "visible shape to the idea that sin leads to more
sin, and that to disaster." He notes that the dochmiacs of the
parodos of the *Seven against Thebes* imply an "uneven method
of progress," expressive of the terror and disorder of the chorus;
"the chorus swirls into the *orchēstra* with a dance which gives
visible shape to the idea of panic." He has expressed the opinion
also that the dances of Sophocles, at least, were probably not
naturalistic, and that the dancers could "portray only a mood or
an ethos." As we shall see later, E. R. Dodds has also given close
attention to the effect of the choral meters.

The lyrics of the odes must have been sung with careful attention to diction (even though Greek theatres had excellent acous-
tics), for their meaning was not always too easy to grasp quickly.
Probably the chorus assisted listeners immeasurably in the comprehension of these odes by their expressive "dancing with the
hands," *cheironomia.* But not all the dancing of the chorus was
of this type; some of it was definitely dancing, in our sense of
the word—and lively dancing, at that.

Frequently short choral songs, not properly *stasima,* are inter-
jected, almost abruptly, into the episodes, usually at a moment
of great excitement or joy. They give the immediate reaction of
the chorus to what is happening, and are very spirited. These
songs seem to have been accompanied with lively dancing and
gesture. Many writers, following a few scholiasts, call these interludes *hyporchēmata.* The *hyporchēma,* native to Crete, was
a rapid, "flashing," "sportive" dance.[27] At times it made use of
two choral groups, one of which sang and used dance gestures or
simple movements, while at the same time another group of

---

[27] Athenaeus 14.630 D-E; Plutarch *Quaest. conv.* 9.15.2.748 A-C.

dancers performed spiritedly without singing. Eventually it seems to have become merely a lively, joyous dance, with strong mimetic gestures. It is apparently in this sense that the word has been applied by scholiasts and by modern scholars to such choral odes as that in Euripides' *Bacchae,* lines 1153-1164, where the leader of the chorus exhorts the group to dance a joyous *kallinikos,* or victory dance; and also to those in Sophocles' *Trachiniae* 205-223 and *Ajax* 693-716. Thus it is entirely possible that a modern scholar might classify a given dance as a *hyporchēma* and as another type of dance—e.g., a victory dance—at the same time.

Often the place of one choral ode is taken by a *kommos*—a powerful and moving dirge, sung usually in alternation by the chorus and one or more actors. We see such a dirge, for example, in the *Persians* of Aeschylus (918-1075), in the *Ajax* of Sophocles (880-973), and in the *Trojan Women* (1227-1255), *Hippolytus* (811-898), *Orestes* (960-1012), and *Suppliants* of Euripides (778-835). The word *kommos* means literally "beating," "striking." Evidently in the *kommos* various gestures were used which recalled the very old custom of beating the breast and the head, raking the cheeks with the fingernails, and tearing the hair, beard, or robes to express grief.[28]

Sometimes, particularly in the plays of Euripides, a character is given a dramatic monody or monologue. Evidently this, too, would be accompanied with appropriate gestures.

Occasionally in the choral odes (or even during an episode) the chorus divides itself into two semi-choruses, opposing each other in thought, or counseling two different courses of action. This division would be reflected in movements and gestures. In like manner, in some of the odes the chorus becomes a group of individuals who relate varying experiences, reveal differing reactions, or even argue with one another.[29] Normally, however, the chorus is really a unit.

It was customary for the chorus to remain on the scene of the action throughout the play; there are, however, a few extant plays (the *Ajax* of Sophocles, for example, and the *Alcestis* and *Helen* of Euripides) in which the chorus leaves and later returns. Prob-

---

28 Cf. Aeschylus *Choeph.* 423-428.
29 Cf. Aeschylus *Agam.* 1346-1371.

ably the chorus withdrew to the background at times, and then advanced when the time came for a greater measure of participation in the action of the play. The whole of the great *orchēstra* was apparently theirs for movement and grouping—a space sometimes as large as seventy feet in diameter.

After the episodes and *stasima* comes the *exodos* or conclusion of the play. It comprises everything from the last choral ode to the end. Usually it consists of the choral ode, then a brief dialogue, and finally a few lines of anapaestic verse, sung by the chorus just before, or as, they march out of the *orchēstra*. Some plays end with elaborate processions and accompanying song—as, e.g., the *Eumenides* of Aeschylus; some, on the other hand, have no exit-lines at all for the chorus—e.g., the *Agamemnon* and *Prometheus Bound* of Aeschylus, and the *Trachiniae* of Sophocles. It was customary, however, for the chorus to leave as it had entered, in rectangular formation, marching.

Occasionally, for the particular exigencies of the play, the poet might introduce a subordinate chorus, in addition to the chorus proper. Examples of this practice are to be seen at the conclusion of the *Eumenides* of Aeschylus, in which a secondary chorus of "escorters" sings as it conducts the Eumenides to their new home; at the conclusion of Aeschylus' *Suppliants,* in which the hand-maidens of the daughters of Danaus unite in song with their mistresses; and near the beginning of the *Hippolytus* of Euripides (61-72), where a supplementary chorus of huntsmen enters with the protagonist, and sings a brief choral ode.[30]

The steps, figures, and gestures of the dance of tragedy were carefully taught to the members of the chorus, and were never left to chance or to the inspiration of the moment. Even the movements of the chorus in the *orchēstra* were plotted beforehand. We have specific record of lines, *grammai,*[31] marked out on the floor of the *orchēstra* to guide the members of the chorus in their evolutions.

Plutarch, in the first-second century of the Christian era, said in one of his essays[32] that there were three elements in the Greek

---

[30] For conjectures on other secondary choruses see Pickard-Cambridge, *Dramatic Festivals* (above, note 5), *passim.*

[31] Hesychius *s.v.* "grammai."

[32] *Quaest. conv.* 9.15.2.747 B-748 E.

dance, viz., *phora, schēma,* and *deixis.* He elaborated at some
length on what he considered the significance of each. Although
his account presents numerous difficulties of interpretation, many
writers from his own day to the present time have endeavored to
follow him in this threefold division of the dance. Inasmuch as
his three terms, and particularly *schēma,* are often used in connection with the dance of tragedy, some brief notice must be
taken of them here. However, it should be borne in mind that Plutarch was writing several centuries after the classical period of
the Greek dance, had never seen the dances of which he wrote,
and was writing as a philosopher, not as a student or historian
of the dance. A scrutiny of the use of his three terms and related
words in Greek writers from the classical period to and beyond
his time yields the following conclusions:[33] The three words are
used in connection with the dance, but they are not precise technical terms for the dance, in any modern, scientific sense; they
are not parallel; and they are not mutually exclusive. They are
all wide in scope, and are used with differing connotations by
different Greek writers and at different periods. In the main, *phora*
denotes "carriage"—the way in which a dancer carries himself,
moves from place to place—a combination, in fact, of our concepts
of "step" and "movement." *Schēma,* which at times apparently over-
laps with *phora,* can mean variously "gesture," "figure," "pose,"
"movement," "pattern of motion," or "picture in the dance." *Deixis,*
which seems to mean "portrayal," "interpretation," "acting out,"
"playing the part of," "representation," appears in Plutarch to
refer also to *cheironomia,* which in the usage of other authors
comprises a body of *schēmata.*

To the dance of tragedy, as we have seen, Phrynichus and many
other writers of tragedy down to and including Aeschylus, at
least,[34] contributed *schēmata* of their own devising. Under these
circumstances it is not surprising to find that ancient authors
mention the names of a large number of formal *schēmata* which
they recognize as characteristic of the tragic dance.

To gain some comprehension of the nature of the dance of
tragedy, it is necessary first to survey briefly such *schēmata* as

---

[33] Lillian B. Lawler, *"Phora, Schēma, Deixis* in the Greek Dance," *Transactions of the American Philological Association,* LXXXV (1954), 148-158.
[34] Athenaeus 1.21 E-F, 22 A; Plutarch *Quaest. conv.* 8.9.3.732 F.

are attested for it. In doing so, however, we must observe some caution. Where Greek writers specifically use the word *emmeleia* in speaking of dances and figures, we are on reasonably safe ground. On the other hand, some writers use instead the adjective *tragikos*. In the case of writers and lexicographers of late antiquity, the word *tragikos* is sometimes used to mean "tragic," but at other times it is used rather loosely. Philoxenus the dithyrambist, for example, is called *tragikos* by a scholiast on Aristophanes' *Plutus* (290). By some late authors the word seems to be used literally, as coming from *tragos*, "goat," and referring to the dances of the satyr play; we may instance *Etymologicum Magnum* 764, *s.v.* "tragoedia," where tragedy and the satyr play are obviously confused, and where the choruses are said at times to imitate the *schēmata* of goats. Many modern scholars think that in the lexicographers the word *tragikos* means merely "pertaining to the drama." In the ensuing pages, the possibility that *tragikos* really means "of tragedy" will be considered in the case of each *schēma* so designated.

We are told by Pollux (4.105) that one of the *schēmata* of the "tragic dance" *(tragikēs orchēseōs)* was something called *parabēnai ta tettara*—"to walk past the four." Latte[35] interprets this as denoting a shifting of position, when the dancers are arranged in five rows of three each, so that those in the last row come forward and become the first row, or those in the first row move to the rear and become the last row, passing four other rows in so doing. He accepts the figure as authentic for the dance of tragedy, when the chorus was composed of fifteen men. This would seem to be a reasonable interpretation, and one which would rule out a reference to the satyr play—for, as we shall see later, the chorus of that type of drama was regularly composed of twelve *choreutae*. In like manner, this interpretation would exclude the *schēma* from the dance of comedy, with its chorus of twenty-four. Such a figure would be eminently suited to the tetragonal *emmeleia* of tragedy, with its suggestion of marching and counter-marching.

Another *schēma* attested by Pollux for the "tragic dance" (4.105), and called in the Hesychius *Lexicon (s.v.)* "a kind of dance," is the *diplē*, "the double." That the figure was used also

---

[35] Kurt Latte, *De Saltationibus Graecorum Capita Quinque* (Giessen, 1913), p. 26.

in comedy is rendered practically certain by a passage in the *Thesmophoriazusae* of Aristophanes (982-984). It may have been similar to the second figure of the dance described in *Iliad* 18.599-601—a figure in which the dancers form two lines and dance in opposition to one another.[36] Such a figure would be, in effect, a temporary division of the chorus into two half-choruses—a division common in the Greek theatre.[37] It might appear, for example, in such passages as the strophe of the choral ode in lines 1036-1058 of Euripides' *Iphigenia at Aulis*. There the chorus, women of Chalcis, recall the dances at the wedding feast of Peleus and Thetis, in which two supernatural groups, the Muses and the Nereids, participated. It would be natural for the chorus to imitate those dances, briefly. The "charm" which Aristophanes associates with the *diplē* (*Thesmo.* 982) would have consisted largely in the rapidity, grace, and subtlety with which the two lines approached, passed, or mingled with each other, or went forward and back, toward and away from each other.

The "flat hand"—*cheir kataprēnēs* or *katapranēs*—is an orchestic *schēma* mentioned as such by Athenaeus (14.630 A). Pollux (4.105) says it is one of the *schēmata* of the "tragic" dance. Evidence from the epic poems[38] and elsewhere would indicate that the Greek words must denote an actual slap with the flat of the hand, directed at some part of the dancer's own person, or at some other person or thing.[39] The slapping of one's own thigh or breast in Greek antiquity denoted distress, grief, displeasure, anger[40]—or, oddly enough, in the case of the thigh, the exact opposite, viz., great glee, as in modern times. The significance of a slap or blow directed at another person would be obvious. There are innumerable ancient representations of dancing figures which

---

[36] Lillian B. Lawler, "*Diplē, Dipodia, Dipodismos* in the Greek Dance," *Transactions of the American Philological Association*, LXXVI (1945), 59-73; cf. Xenophon *Anab.* 5.4.12.

[37] Pollux 4.107.

[38] *Iliad* 15.113-114; 397-398; 16.792; *Odyssey* 13.164, 199.

[39] Lillian B. Lawler, "Flat Hand in the Greek Dance," *Classical Outlook*, XIX (1942), 58-60; "*Airein Maschalēn* and Associated Orchestic *Schēmata*," *Transactions of the American Philological Association*, LXXX (1949), 230-237; Ervin Roos, *Die tragische Orchestik im Zerrbild der altattischen Komödie* (Lund, 1951), p.90, regards this *schēma* and also the following one, *simē cheir*, as purely satyric.

[40] Sittl (above, note 13), pp. 12, 20, 25.

show a slapping gesture. Evidently the *schēma* was used freely in tragedy, comedy, and the satyr play. In tragedy there is ample opportunity for the use of the figure, in both its forms. In the *kommos* particularly, and elsewhere also, members of the chorus could slap their own thighs or chests to denote deep grief. In a great many of the extant Greek tragedies there are passages in which the chorus actually does strike, or at least threatens to strike, one of the characters;[41] here the gesture could also be used.

Of a somewhat similar nature is *simē cheir,* attested as "tragic" in Pollux (4.105) and the Hesychius *Lexicon (s.v.),* and as a *schēma* by Athenaeus (14.630 A) and Hesychius. The adjective *simē* literally means "snub-nosed." When applied to the hand, as in the name of our *schēma,* it seems to denote "bent upwards"— i.e., a hand held in such a way that there is tension in it, and the fingers, out at full length, curve up, back, and away from the palm. This gesture could be seen in a hand held in many positions—palm down, palm toward the dancer's body, palm away from the dancer's body, hand before the dancer's face, hand behind the dancer's back, etc. It would seem to be, then, something not un-like the characteristic hand gesture of the Cambodian ritual dances, as seen today, but without the excessive, abnormal tension of the fingers which long professional training in those dances has given to the Oriental performers. Perhaps no gesture is de-picted so often as this, in Greek art and particularly on Greek vases. It was in common use in everyday Greek life. Furthermore, it seems to have had a varying significance, according to varying circumstances. It is seen in representations of ordinary conversa-tions, as well as of "revel" dances, funeral dances, and ritual dances of various sorts. It seems to have been especially common in Di-onysiac dances and in the satyr play, as well as in tragedy. A care-ful study of several hundred representations of the gesture[42] shows that it can be used to express (1) muscular tension; (2) rapidity of motion; (3) worship or deference to a statue, an altar, etc.; (4) surprise; (5) marked admiration; (6) pointing; (7) mimetic

---

[41] E.g., probably in the *hymnos desmios* in Aeschylus' *Eumenides* 307-396; in Sophocles' *Oed. Col.* 824, 833-847; in Euripides' *Iph. Taur.* 798-799.

[42] Lillian B. Lawler, "A 'Snub-Nosed' Hand in the Greek Dance," *Classical Outlook,* XX (1943), 70-72; "The Maenads," *Memoirs of the American Academy in Rome,* VI (1927), 96-100.

carrying of an imaginary object on the palm of the hand; (8) abandon; (9) deterrence; (10) caution or stealth. In conversation it probably had the significance of pointing or emphasizing. Among all the uses of the gesture, the "deterrence" significance, especially when the tensed hand is held before the face, palm out, is probably the most important. Greek tragedy, of course, abounds in horrible or terrifying episodes, and also in accounts of such episodes, related by messengers or others. Naturally the observers or listeners in these cases would react to the horror or terror of the situation—and how more naturally than with this *schēma*? It could be used in tragedy when a horrible sight is revealed, or upon the apparition of a divinity or of other supernatural beings, or at the crashing and flashing of heaven-sent thunder and lightning. Specifically, it could be used at the close of the *Choephorae* of Aeschylus (1048-1062), when Orestes sees the Furies and recoils from them; in Sophocles' *Oedipus the King* (1297-1307), where the chorus turns away in deep distress so as not to see the blinded eyes of the king; in Euripides' *Trojan Women* (307-340), where the chorus must have turned in sorrow from the pathos of Cassandra's "wedding song"; in Euripides' *Orestes* (819-843), where the chorus details how Orestes killed his mother; and in innumerable other plays in which the chorus recounts, or hears of, scenes of horror. We recall, in connection with all the passages cited, that interpretative gestures, even in non-orchestic portions of a play, were regarded by the Greeks as a form of dancing. It is easy to see how this figure came to be considered an eminently appropriate one for tragedy.

Still another *schēma*, named by Athenaeus (14.630 A), and associated by Pollux (4.105) with the "tragic dance," is one called *xylou paralēpsis*. The words seem to denote "taking hold of the wood." There has been much discussion as to the significance of such a name in the dance. The best explanation would seem to be that it implies a real or symbolic taking up or using of a wooden club or staff, in an enactment of beating or threatened violence.[43]

---

[43] Lillian B. Lawler, "Beating Motifs in the Greek Dance," *Classical Outlook*, XXI (1944), 59-61. Dean Harry L. Levy, of the City University of New York, has kindly corroborated my interpretation of this *schēma* by adducing the parallel of the modern Greek threat, "Tha phas xylo"—literally, "You will eat wood"—customarily addressed by a parent to an erring youngster,

In Aristophanes' *Wasps* 458 Bdelycleon bids Xanthias beat the wasps with a club—*paie tō xylō*. In Greek tragedy many characters and many choruses would normally carry a staff—e.g., all old men, blind men, seers, wise men, priests, heralds, messengers, suppliants, beggars, shepherds, or even certain deities. It would be difficult indeed, to imagine a Greek play of any sort which would not have in it at least one of the types mentioned. For an actor or a member of the chorus actually bearing a staff or club in his hand to brandish it for a mimetic blow during the course of the play would be entirely normal, and a mimetic or threatened blow with a real or imaginary staff could occur with any type of character or chorus. Among the many non-orchestic passages in which the *schēma* would be fairly certain to appear are e.g., the king's threat to the herald in Aeschylus' *Suppliants* (925) and the herald's threat to the chorus (836-842); the chorus' attempt to drive Oedipus away, in Sophocles' *Oedipus at Colonus* (227); Peleus' defiance of Menelaus in Euripides' *Andromache* (588); and, in the *Hercules Furens* of Euripides (254-256), the coryphaeus' exhortation to the rest of the chorus to raise their staffs against Lycus. Greek drama—tragedy, comedy, and the satyr play—is amazingly rich in scenes of violence or threatened violence. It is not impossible that this element in the drama may stem ultimately from primitive ritual. Ceremonial beatings and beating dances are in general of two well-known types—those performed to induce fertility, and those performed to drive out evil spirits. Both types would have a place in the worship of Dionysus.

A *schēma* mentioned often by Greek writers,[44] and by some of them positively associated with the *emmeleia*,[45] is the "sword" figure—*xiphismos*—or "the sword thrust"—*xiphizein, apoxiphizein.* Variant terms for it are *xiphisma, skiphizein, skiphismos.* However, the connotation of passages in which the figure is discussed

---

with the accompaniment of a strong "chopping" gesture. For the "taking" of something in the hand by the leader of a dancing chorus see Sophron, frag. 156, Kaibel, ap. Athenaeus 8.362 C. There have been other interpretations of the *schēma.*

[44] Pollux 4.99; Athenaeus 14.629 F; Suidas *s.v.* "xiphizein"; Hesychius *s.vv.* "xiphizein," "xiphismatōn," "skiphizei"; *Et. Mag.* 611.10.

[45] Hesychius *s.vv.* "xiphismos," "apoxiphizein"; Suidas and Photius *s.v.* "xiphismos"; Pausanias, frag. 264, Schwabe; Eustathius 1167.23 and 1604.51.

is frequently[46] suggestive of an obscene dance. Scholars have debated at some length[47] the exact significance of this figure. The obvious conclusion would seem to be that the figure originally was a mimetic sword thrust with the hand, used in tragedy by either actors or chorus, during the recounting of a tale of combat or slaying (as in Aeschylus' *Seven against Thebes* 888-899 and 911-914; Sophocles' *Ajax* 228-240 and *Antigone* 1232-1233; Euripides' *Andromache* 1118-1119 and 1150; *Hecuba* 567 and 1161-1162; *Iphigenia among the Taurians* 296-300 and 322; and the pseudo-Euripidean *Rhesus* 794-795), or when an actor or the chorus threatens or incites to violence (as in Aeschylus' *Agamemnon* 1651 and *Suppliants* 839-841; Euripides' *Orestes* 1302-1305 and 1349-1350; and the *Rhesus* 675-687); but that in later times the gesture of the thrust of the hand, especially under the cloak, acquired an obscene significance, and was used in that sense in comedy and the satyr play. In tragedy, we may assume that the figure was used either by the speaker or by the chorus, the latter listening and accompanying the spoken word with gesture.

Another *schēma* which has been much discussed is that called the *kalathiskos* or *kalathismos*.[48] Pollux specifically designates it as "of the tragic dance"—*tragikēs orchēseōs*. Athenaeus (11.467 F), quoting Apollophanes, calls the *kalathiskos* a "kind of dance," and couples it with the *deinos* or *dinos,* a dance characterized by much violent whirling. Later (14.629F) Athenaeus includes among the *schēmata* of the dance one called the *kalathismos*, putting it after the *xiphismos*. A few lines farther on (14.630 A) he lists the *kalathiskos* in the same sentence with the *schēmata* known as *cheir kataprēnēs, cheir simē,* and *xylou paralēpsis*—as does Pollux (4.105)—and with the *strobilos*, a whirling figure, perhaps similar or equivalent to the *deinos*. In the Hesychius *Lexicon* (*s.v.*) the *kalathiskos* is defined merely as a "kind of dance."

The word *kalathiskos*, of course, denotes a reed basket, of the type used by women for wool and for household objects. It is a diminutive of *kalathos,* "basket"—a word which is itself used as

46 Pollux 4.99; Athenaeus 14.629 F.
47 Latte (above, note 35), p. 18; Heinz Schnabel, *Kordax* (Munich, 1910), pp. 4-5; Roos (above, note 39), pp. 164-165; Lillian B. Lawler and Alice E. Kober. "The Thracian Pig Dance," *Classical Philology*, XL (1945), 100, 104.
48 Pollux 4.105.

an orchestic term. Eustathius (1627.46-50), speaks of baskets of Demeter "which, the story goes, dance in certain mysteries of Demeter." Strabo, writing of the famous temple of the Coloenian Artemis in Lydia, remarks (13.4.5.626); "And they say that here, at the festivals, the baskets (tous kalathous) dance—though I do not know why they tell such fantastic tales rather than speak the truth."

The basket played a part in the worship of Dionysus, and also of various goddesses, notably Artemis, Demeter, Athena, and, to a lesser extent, Aphrodite. Priestesses and attendants of these divinities, in cult rituals, often carried baskets on their heads; and for a maiden to be chosen "basket-bearer" in a festal procession was a high honor. It is possible that in some cults these maidens may have danced—or the procession itself may have been thought of as a dance. In any case, the expression "the baskets dance" might have arisen naturally, as a metaphorical usage for "the maidens carrying baskets dance."

Some scholars have held that the kalathiskos is a brief figure of the tragic dance in which the dancer, using one hand or both hands, reaches up in a graceful gesture as if steadying a real or imaginary basket on his or her head.[49] Others refer all three terms—kalathos, kalathiskos, kalathismos—to the mysterious "dancing reeds" which Isigonus (frag. 8) says dance at an annual festival at Lake Tala, in Lydia.[50] Still others refer the terms to the famous dances of the maidens of Caryae, a Laconian city on the borders of Arcadia. Athenaeus says that the tragic and satyric poet Pratinas wrote a play called Dumainai or Karyatides (9.392 F). The Caryatid dances had apparently originated in the cult of a local tree goddess, Karyatis, who in time coalesced with Artemis.[51] Still later, Dionysiac elements entered the cult. The dancers seem to have worn characteristic headdresses, perhaps made of the leaves of the sacred tree.

Most modern commentators cite the many representations on vases, reliefs, coins, gems, etc., from the fifth century through the

---

[49] Latte (above, note 35), p. 17.
[50] A. B. Cook, Zeus (Cambridge, 1914-1940), III, 975-1015.
[51] Paul Wolters, "Karyatiden," Zeitschrift für bildende Kunst, Neue Folge, VI (1895), 36-44; Théophile Homolle, "L'Origine des Caryatides," Revue Archéologique, 5th Series, Tome V (1917), 1-67.

Hellenistic and Roman periods, which depict girls, and some boys as well, wearing reed-like or basket-shaped headdresses, as they engage in a spirited dance. These little figures are usually clad in short, light chitons; but some of the male figures, especially the late examples, are nude, and other male figures wear women's dresses, long or short. For the most part the dancers step daintily on the balls of the feet, use graceful gestures of the hand and arm, lower their heads modestly, and apparently whirl or turn frequently. Among the figures are many in company with Dionysus, Maenads, and satyrs. Some of the latter, indeed, look very much as if they are burlesquing the ritual basket-bearing figures. It is possible that Pollux in this connection is using *tragikos* loosely, to denote "satyric" as well as "tragic." There is some evidence that "the basket" may really have been a *schēma* of the satyr drama, in which the beautiful basket dances of cult ritual were burlesqued. We shall discuss this possibility later.

Pollux (4.105) lists also among *schēmata* of the "tragic" dance the *thermaustris,* or "fire-tongs." Elsewhere (4.102) he uses both the word *thermaustris* and its plural, *thermaustrides,* as the name of a separate dance, which he says was lively, and characterized by leaping. Athenaeus mentions the *thermaustris* among *schēmata* of the dance (14.630 A), and also among dances which are *maniōdeis*—i.e., like the dance of a madman (14.629 D-E). Photius (*s.v.*) and the *Lexicon* of Hesychius (*s.v.*) say it was "violent," "fiery," and noted for its speed. Lucian (*Salt.* 34) mentions *thermaustrizein* as a figure, but passes over it as having no bearing on the Greco-Roman pantomimic dance, with which he is primarily concerned. Eustathius (1601.27), quoting Critias, gives us our most extended account of the *thermaustris.* It is violent, he says; the dancers leap high up and cross their feet several times in the air before they descend to the ground. The attendant openings and closings of the legs undoubtedly gave the figure its name. Eustathius, still quoting Critias, says that the *schēma* was associated with ball-playing. Inasmuch as Critias was the author of a treatise on the constitution of the Lacedaemonians, many scholars think he must have mentioned this orchestic *schēma* as distinctively Spartan. It is well known, to be sure, that the Spartans delighted in ball-playing, and in physical skill in general; yet the use of the ball-dance in the *Odyssey* (8.370-384) would indicate that both

[41]

102,544

the dance and the *schēma* were familiar to all the Greeks from earliest times. We recall that a ball-dance, performed by the playwright himself, is definitely attested for a tragedy based on the *Odyssey*—the *Nausicaä* of Sophocles.[52]

Immediately after the *thermaustris* in his list of "tragic" *schēmata*, Pollux (4.105) places *kybistēsis*, or tumbling. Rhythmic tumbling seems to have been associated with the dance from the time of the Minoans—who, in fact, were said to have been the "inventors" of both.[53] Certainly acrobatics and tumbling were features of festivals, wedding and other processions, after-dinner entertainment, and joyous gatherings in general, all through antiquity. The *kybistēsis* is similar in nature to the *thermaustris,* which is near it in Pollux's list. It may not be amiss to cite here the parallel of grand opera, which often admits very spirited and even acrobatic dances into very tragic stories.

An early commentator on the *Wasps* of Aristophanes[54] informs us that a figure known as *skelos rhiptein,* or a "high kick," was found in the "tragic dance."[55] It may indeed have been used on occasion in tragedy, in passages where such other figures as the *thermaustris* and *kybistēsis* were introduced. However, from the nature of the figure one may suspect that it is attested as tragic from the passage in the *Wasps* alone; and, as we shall see, that particular passage deals obviously with a burlesque. Elsewhere the figure seems to appear in comedy.[56]

There are other *schēmata*, not positively identified as tragic by ancient authors, but which may nevertheless have been used in tragedy. A few of these may be considered briefly.

Pollux (4.105) describes a figure which he calls *schistas helkein,* in which "it was necessary for the dancer, leaping, to interchange his legs." The *Lexicon* of Hesychius seems to refer to the same or a similar figure under the name *schisma*. In each case the Greek word denotes a "split," and the figure would seem to be similar to the modern dancing and acrobatic figure of that name. Evidently the dancer leaped high, interchanged his legs quickly with

---

[52] Athenaeus 1.20 F.
[53] Athenaeus 5.181 B.
[54] Schol. *Wasps* 1530.
[55] See Roos (above, note 39), pp. 82, 89, 97, 104, 168-178.
[56] Cf. Aristophanes *Peace* 332.

the knees held stiff, and descended to the floor with one leg out straight in the front and the other out straight in the rear. The general resemblance of this figure to the *thermaustris* and the *kybistēsis* would indicate a possible use in tragedy along with those figures.

It is well known that the Greeks, in praying to or invoking a divinity or other supernatural being, made use of characteristic gestures and motions.[57] Since in tragedy the chorus or a character frequently prays to a deity, it is reasonable to conclude that such gestures and motions had an important place in the performances. Normally a Greek when praying to a god (except chthonic divinities) stood, raised his eyes to the heavens, and stretched his arms aloft, palms up. Such a gesture would be used appropriately, e.g., by the chorus in Sophocles' *Oedipus the King*, 151-215, as it prays to Artemis, Athena, Zeus, Apollo, and Dionysus; by the chorus in the same playwright's *Philoctetes*, 391-402, as it calls upon the mother of Zeus; by the chorus in the *Ion* of Euripides, praying to Athena and Artemis (452-491); by the chorus in the *Orestes* of Euripides, 352-359, as it appeals to Zeus, and, in the same play, 316-331, as it implores the Furies—here specifically spoken of as soaring through the upper air. Sometimes in supplication the members of the chorus may throw themselves at the feet of statues of the gods, or even clasp the statues, as in the *Seven against Thebes* of Aeschylus, 94-97. In praying to divinities of the earth and the lower world, the Greeks turned their palms downward, or, more urgently, sat or cast themselves on the ground and beat the earth with hands or feet. Such a *schēma* might appear, e.g., in the *Persians* of Aeschylus, 627-680 (cf. also 683), where the chorus invokes Earth, Hermes, the Lord of the Dead, and the ghost of Darius; in the *Ion* of Euripides, 1048-1060, where the chorus calls upon Hecate; and in the *Trojan Women* of Euripides, 1304-1310, where Hecuba casts herself on the ground and beats the earth with her hands, while the members of the chorus kneel about her, all of them calling upon the dead.

In imploring a favor of a person, a Greek, at least in the early period of his history, might kneel before him, and perhaps clasp his knees or his beard. In tragedy, a petitioner might act similarly.

---

[57] Sittl (above, note 13), pp. 174-199.

Such *schēmata* could be used, e.g., by the chorus throughout the *Suppliants* of Aeschylus and of Euripides, in both orchestic and non-orchestic situations; and by such characters as, for example, Molossus in the *Andromache* of Euripides, 528-536.

In representations in Cretan and Greek art there appears a gesture of shielding the eyes, oddly like the modern military salute. In some cases this gesture has been interpreted, correctly, I believe, as an example of a ritualistic shielding of the eyes from the radiance of a deity.[58] A similar gesture, known variously as the *skopos, aposkopōn,* and *hyposkopos cheir,* and used in a *schēma* of "peering," is found frequently in representations of satyrs, and will be discussed more fully in connection with the satyr play. Athenaeus (14.630 A) lists the *skopos* with five other *schēmata* which Pollux in a parallel passage (4.105) specifically labels "tragic." Such a gesture could have a wide usage in tragedy. It might appear at any point in an orchestic or non-orchestic situation where the members of the chorus look off-scene toward a particular place or an approaching person—as, e.g., in Aeschylus' *Agamemnon* 493-498; Euripides' *Bacchae* 1164; and Euripides' *Alcestis* 234-235—or definitely seek a person or thing, as in Sophocles' *Oedipus at Colonus* 118-137 and Euripides' *Orestes* 1251-1293, or, even more strikingly, in the spectacular "trailing" song of the chorus in Aeschylus' *Eumenides* 245-276. The shielding of the eyes against radiance could be used effectively in every tragedy in which a divinity appears, or in which a character of particular radiance is introduced. Especially appropriate for it would be a passage in the *Persians* of Aeschylus (150-152) in which the chorus likens the radiance of the queen to that of the gods.

We have noted that in the *kommos* Greek tragedy apparently makes use of characteristic *schēmata* and gestures to express grief—beating the head and breast, and tearing the cheeks, the hair, the beard, the garments. These were undoubtedly used not only in the *kommos,* but elsewhere in the plays as well—as, e.g., in choral passages in the *Choephorae* (22-31) and the *Persians*

---

[58] Otto Kern, *Die Religion der Griechen* (Berlin, 1926), I, 25; E. S. McCartney, "The Blinding Radiance of the Divine Visage," *Classical Journal,* XXXVI (1941), 485-488; Lillian B. Lawler, "Blinding Radiance and the Greek Dance," *Classical Journal,* XXXVII (1941), 94-96.

(120-125) of Aeschylus, the *Ajax* of Sophocles (631-633), and the *Trojan Women* (1235-1236, 1251-1256) and *Suppliants* (41-86 and especially 71-78) of Euripides. In the *Suppliants* these mourning *schēmata* are actually called a dance—"the only dance which Hades respects." They are found also in connection with Euripides' famous dramatic monodies (cf. *Orestes* 960-1012, *Trojan Women* 279-291). Other *schēmata* of grief, familiar from Greek art, were probably used—bowing the head, resting the palm on the top of the head, drawing the cloak or veil over the face, stretching the hands towards the object of grief or pity, and even sinking and beating upon the ground (*Trojan Women* 1304-1308).

In his fourteenth book, Athenaeus says (14.629 F): "And to the flute they danced the dance of the *keleustēs* . . . ." The Greek *keleustēs* or boatswain was the officer whose duty it was to keep the rowers pulling together in rhythm. That the activities of the *keleustēs* may not have been too simple, or purely formal, is attested by a famous story:[59] When Alcibiades returned to Athens, victorious after a naval battle, in a ship with purple sails, his *keleustēs* was Callipides, one of the most famous of Greek tragic actors, and for him the great musician Chrysogonus, winner at the Pythian games, played the flute. The dance of the *keleustēs* undoubtedly contained a *schēma* suggestive of the rhythm of rowing. As a matter of fact, the actual motion of rowing must in itself have seemed a sort of dance to the Greeks, because of its rhythmical nature, and because it was often actually done to music. There seems clear evidence in the extant plays that a *schēma* of "rowing" had a place in tragedy.[60] In choral passages of all three of the great tragic poets oars and rowing are often mentioned. Euripides in his *Electra* (432-441) has a choral passage in which the ships of the Achaeans, with their oar-strokes, are said to "dance" with the Nereids and dolphins; and in the *Helen* (1451-1456) he calls the oar of a ship the *chorēgus* of the dancing dolphins. Especially striking are lines 1123-1136 of the same poet's *Iphigenia among the Taurians*, in which the chorus sings of the fifty-oared ship which will carry the heroine and her two companions back to Greece, and for which Pan himself, with his reed pipe, and Apollo,

---

[59] Athenaeus 12.535 D.

[60] Lillian B. Lawler, "A Figure of the Tragic Dance," *Classical Bulletin*, XXVII (1950), 3-4.

with his lyre, are to serve as *keleustai* to the rowers. And not only in choral passages are oars and rowing mentioned; very often one of the characters speaks of them. In short, it is something of a commonplace in Greek tragedy for an actor or the chorus to sing of the plying of oars, as some person or group of persons is borne across the sea.

In addition to the passages we have considered, there are others in which the reference to oars or rowing is metaphorical in significance, and is associated with the expression of grief. In Aeschylus' *Seven against Thebes,* for instance (854-860), the *coryphaeus* bids the chorus, in giving vent to its sorrow, to imitate in gesture the rowing of the ship of the dead. This, incidentally, is the most specific reference which we have to a possible rowing *schēma* in tragedy. In the *Persians* of Aeschylus (1046) Xerxes, leading the sorrowful chant of the chorus, says "Row, row, and moan for my sake." The chorus apparently obeys, for its next line is a wail of lamentation. In the *Choephorae* of the same author (425-428), the chorus seems to speak of similar "rowing" motions about the head to accompany its wailing. Evidently the striking of the head in grief could be called, figuratively, "rowing."

It is possible, then, that a schematized figure or gesture of rowing had a place in the dance of tragedy, and that it had two uses—one to accompany an actual mention of rowing, the other as a symbolical expression of grief.

There are in Greek tragedy a great many bird similes, and a great number of references to birds and flying—many more than could be accounted purely the result of chance. Examples are seen frequently in the works of Euripides, and in almost every case they involve women. Apparently in Euripides it is a commonplace to have a chorus of women, in a choral ode, express the wish that they might become birds, or might have wings, to fly away (cf. *Hippolytus* 732-737; *Helen* 1479-1487; *Iph. Taur.* 1089-1105 and 1139-1142). Aeschylus and Sophocles use similar motifs, but somewhat less extensively, in the extant plays (cf. Aeschylus, *Suppliants* 223-225; Sophocles, *Oed. Col.* 1079-1081, *Ajax* 167-171). In all these passages a "bird" or "flying" *schēma* or gesture might be used, and it is possible that some such *schēma* had a place in the dance of tragedy.

We have been considering some of the formations, movements,

and *schēmata* characteristic of the dance of tragedy, or probably to be associated with it. Entirely apart from these, it would seem from even the most cursory reading of the plays that there are included in them a rich array of dances of many sorts, appropriate in one way or another to the story of the play. Frequently in these cases the *coryphaeus* or some other person announces that a dance is now to be performed (as in Euripides' *Electra* 859-865) or exhorts the chorus or others to dance with him (as in Aeschylus' *Eumenides* 307; Sophocles' *Antigone* 152-153; Euripides' *Hercules Furens* 761-764, and *Trojan Women* 332-334)—sometimes even calling upon a deity or the Muses to join in or lead the dance (as in Sophocles' *Ajax* 696-701 and *Antigone* 153-154, and in Euripides' *Hercules Furens* 785-789).

Among dances of this sort are various hymn-like processions in which the gods are addressed, invoked, or honored. For instance, the solemn *paean* of Greek ritual is often imitated—as in Sophocles' *Trachiniae* 205-223, and in Euripides' *Ion* 111-143 and *Hercules Furens* 687-694. The hymn of supplication to deities or other divine beings is common (cf. Aeschylus, *Suppliants* 524-537; Euripides, *Medea* 1251-1260 and *Orestes* 316-347), as is also the hymn of gratitude and joy (cf. Aeschylus' *Suppliants* 625-709). In real life such hymns were often accompanied by a solemn, measured walk, or by rhythmic gestures. Here we may recall that the ancient Greek almost never sang or chanted verse without using an accompanying movement of some part of his body.

In some cases the *exodos* of the play itself takes the form of a processional hymn (as in Aeschylus' *Suppliants* 1018-1073; Euripides' *Ion* 1619-1622). Akin to this is the march and chant of the *propompoi*, the attendants sent by Athena to escort the Furies to their new home in Athens, at the conclusion of the *Eumenides* of Aeschylus (1033-1047). Similar also is the funeral procession which is introduced into some plays (as in Euripides' *Suppliants* 778-835; apparently also in *Alcestis* 741-746), or with which some plays end. Aeschylus' *Seven against Thebes*, for example, evidently ends (1059-1084) with two such processions, the chorus dividing to follow the two corpses. The participants in such processions would, of course, make use of the *schēmata* of mourning, which we have already considered.

As we have already noted, victory dances of one sort or another

[47]

occasionally appear in tragedy. In the *Antigone* of Sophocles (148-154), the chorus call for a communal night-long dance to celebrate the Theban victory—and presumably they perform a little of such a dance themselves. In the *Hercules Furens* of Euripides there are two instances of the *kallinikos*. This was a song and dance primarily in honor of Heracles the Victor.[61] In the play, the members of the chorus, old men of Thebes, say (673-681) that, aged as they are, they will continue to sing (and presumably dance) the *kallinikos* in honor of Heracles; later (763-789) they call upon the Nymphs to join with them in their dance-song of victory. The adjective *kallinikos* is applied to Heracles several times in the play. In the *Trachiniae* of Sophocles (205-223) there is an outburst of joy, apparently with a brief dance, when the chorus of women learn of the victory of Heracles over the Oechalians; later, when the members of the chorus expect Heracles to return soon, there is a song and dance (633-662) which definitely seems to form a *kallinikos*, although that word is not used (cf. 644-646). In the *Electra* of Euripides (859-865; 873-879; cf. 880-881) the *kallinikos* is performed by the chorus of women in honor of Orestes after he has slain Aegisthus. In the *Bacchae* of Euripides, Dionysus is called Kallinikos after his victory over Pentheus (1147); and the song and dance in honor of that same victory are spoken of together as the *kallinikos* (1161).

The *kallinikos* was one of the *kōmos* group of dances;[62] the *kōmos* was essentially a processional dance through the streets, with music, song, laughter, and shouting. It is interesting that Pollux (4.105) mentions a *schēma* called the *tetrakōmos* (the "four-sided" or rectangular *kōmos*) immediately after his list of "tragic" figures. The Hesychius *Lexicon* mentions the same *schēma* (*s.v.*), and adds that it was sacred to Heracles the Victor, and was called also *tessares kōmoi*, "four *kōmoi*." There seem to have been various forms of the *kallinikos* and of the *tetrakōmos*. The *kallinikos* could be performed by men, by women, or by men and women alternating in a line; its choreography could be that of a freely-moving procession, of a winding, snake-like line, or of a tetragonal

---

[61] Pollux 4.100; Hesychius *s.v.*; cf. Athenaeus 14.618 C; Lillian B. Lawler, "*Orchēsis Kallinikos*," *Transactions of the American Philological Association*, LXXIX (1948), 254-267.
[62] Lawler, "*Orchēsis Kallinikos*," (above, note 61).

group. One form of the *tetrakōmos* was presumably a *kōmos* in which the participants walked or danced in a rectangular alignment, with the same number of persons abreast in each line. It may well be that the *tetrakōmos* was one kind of *kallinikos*—the very kind, indeed, suited to the chorus of tragedy, with its normally rectangular arrangement.

In the prologue of the *Agamemnon* of Aeschylus there is a passage which has given rise to much discussion. The watchman, seeing the signal-fire that indicates that Troy has fallen, says that he will hasten to inform Clytemnestra of the news, and that if Troy has indeed fallen, "I shall myself dance a prelude" (31). Some editors say that he thereupon performs a dance, or a portion of a dance, upon the rooftop.[63] But it is doubtful if Aeschylus would permit him to slow up the beginning of the play with much of a dance at this point. The difficulties of the passage are complicated by the fact that the watchman's speech is in general colloquial and metaphorical; the lines immediately following, for example, make use of the metaphor of a lucky throw of dice. A scholiast on the passage confused matters still further by adding to the Greek word for "prelude" in the manuscript the words "before Clytemnestra." To clarify the sentence we must go back a few lines. The beacon, says the watchman (23-24), portends the "setting up of many dances" in Argos—in other words, when its message of the fall of Troy becomes known there will be many dances in celebration of the victory, all through the land. I believe that the watchman at line 31 simply cuts a caper or two in anticipation of the coming dances. If the scholiast's addition of the words "before Clytemnestra" is valid, the reference would probably be to the animated gestures with which the watchman will later inform the queen of the victory—much as messengers in tragedy use gestures to accompany their lengthy reports of off-scene happenings.

Dances of the type foreshadowed for Argos in the watchman's speech are partly in the nature of the communal victory dance, partly in that of the communal dance of joy. The latter is not per-

---

[63] George Thomson, *The Oresteia of Aeschylus* (Cambridge, 1938), I, 103; II, 7; cf. also Joseph E. Harry, *Greek Tragedy* (New York, 1933), I, 52-53. Edouard Fraenkel, in *Aeschylus—Agamemnon* (Oxford, 1950), II, 19, summarizes the various interpretations that have been offered.

formed necessarily for a victory; for instance, in Euripides' *Alcestis* (1154-1158), communal dances are ordered by Admetus in celebration of the return of Alcestis. In real life such dances often lasted through the night.

There is indicated in the Greek drama another kind of victory dance—what I have elsewhere[64] called the *hōs epi nīkē* type ("thus for victory"), from the words used in the accompanying song in two extant comedies—the *Ecclesiazusae* (1182) and *Lysistrata* (1293) of Aristophanes. In it the chorus marches or dances while singing a very brief prayer for victory in the dramatic contest. It is found more frequently in comedy than in tragedy, but it does appear in both genres. Often it comes at the end of the play—as in the identical conclusions of the *Orestes* (1691-1693), *Iphigenia among the Taurians* (1497-1499), and *Phoenician Women* (1764-1766) of Euripides; there it is usually interpreted as a plea to the judges for a dramatic victory. The recessional of the chorus in these plays may have been patterned somewhat after the *tetrakōmos* or the *kallinikos;* it would then be hoped that by a sort of "sympathetic magic" it might "induce" a real victory procession!

In the *Ajax* of Sophocles (695-716), the chorus of mariners perform a dance of joy for Ajax's return to sanity. They call upon Pan and the Delian Apollo to lead them in spontaneous dances, Nyssian or Cnossian— that is, Cretan. The whole passage is reminiscent of the winding dances done on Delos by mariners, and may actually reproduce one of those dances. Most of them were probably ultimately of Cretan origin. Frequently the Delian dances, in particular the one known as the *geranos*, were dances of joy and thanksgiving.[65] Other dances of joy are common in tragedy—as, e.g., in the *Hercules Furens* of Euripides, upon the death of Lycus (763-797). Some of them, as we have seen, are apparently of the *hyporchēma* type.

A simple and graceful dance of women, an imitation of what was thought to be the dance of the Nereids, the Muses, the Graces, or other supernatural beings, is apparently introduced briefly into some choral odes—as e.g., in the *Ion* (492-509) of Euripides, and

---

[64] Lawler, *"Orchēsis Kallinikos"* (above, note 61), 257-258.
[65] Lillian B. Lawler, "The Dance of the Ancient Mariners," *Transactions of the American Philological Association,*LXXV (1944), 20-33; also "The *Geranos* Dance," *ibid.,* LXXVII (1946), 112-130.

the *Helen* (1339-1352) of the same author. Also, a wedding dance is found occasionally—as perhaps in Euripides' *Iphigenia among the Taurians* (1140-1151), where the women of the chorus, expressing their longing to return home and join in nuptial dances, probably imitate them briefly. The pathetic dance of Cassandra in Euripides' *Trojan Women* (307-340), in which she bids Hecuba and the chorus to join is, so to speak, a wedding dance in a minor key.

The ecstatic dance of women in honor of Dionysus, with its wild running, whirling, shouting, tossing of hair and of torches and *thyrsi*, frenzied "possession" and ultimate collapse of the dancer, is imitated or suggested frequently—most extensively in the *Bacchae* of Euripides, but very briefly in other plays as well, as, e.g., in the *Antigone* of Sophocles (1115-1151) and the *Helen* (1358-1368) of Euripides. Such a dance, a reversion to primitive rites in honor of Dionysus, would have a peculiar appropriateness in the Dionysiac theatre.

One of the most striking of all the dances in Greek tragedy is the mystic, "lyreless" binding dance of the chorus of Furies in the *Eumenides* of Aeschylus (307-396). It is introduced with seven lines addressed to Orestes, the intended victim, who is informed that while still living he will "furnish a feast" to the Furies, and that he will now hear a *hymnos* which will "bind" him by its magic power. There follows an "invitation to the dance"—"Come now, let us join in the dance" (307). In the ensuing thirteen lines the *choreutae* evidently move into position. The lines accompanying the dance proper (321-396) fall into the following pattern: strophe alpha, ephymnion alpha, antistrophe alpha, ephymnion alpha; strophe beta, ephymnion beta, antistrophe beta, ephymnion beta; strophe gamma, ephymnion gamma, antistrophe gamma, ephymnion gamma; strophe delta, antistrophe delta. The invocation is addressed to Night, mother of the Furies (321-322). The ephymnia, or incantation-like refrains, seek to bind the soul of the victim, to cause him to waste away, to fall, to be crazed. The members of the chorus themselves speak of their figurative descent upon him as "heavy-footed" (*barypesē*, line 372)—an adjective which may have been reflected in their dance. The choreography of the dance may have been in general circular—as in many incantation dances, among varied peoples. The gestures must have

[51]

been threatening and terrifying, and the garments and masks must have combined with them to give an effect of savagery. Some scholars see in the whole passage an echo of real incantations, *katadeseis*, and perhaps of mystic dances which had a place in the cults of deities of darkness and in Orphic magic.

In addition to dances and dance figures which apparently were executed in the course of the plays, Greek tragedies, particularly those of Euripides, often contain striking word pictures of other dances. Even apart from their poetic beauty, such passages are frequently of great value as furnishing us with a vivid glimpse of particular dances, as performed (or imagined) by the Greeks themselves. Among these are the all-night dances and songs of young girls on the hills, in honor of the Matēr Despoina (Euripides, *Heracleidae* 777-783); the dance to Artemis in which Euripides says that Trojan maidens were engaged when the Greeks burst into Troy (*Trojan Women* 551-559); the dance which Hecuba led as queen of Troy, leaning on the scepter of Priam (*Id.* 149-152). Also, Euripides has given us several unforgettable "metaphorical dances": the grim "dance" of the mad Heracles (*Hercules Furens* 878-879, 890-892); the "fluteless dance" which Ares leads, as god of war (*Phoenician Women* 784-797); the horribly punning "pyrrhic" dance of Pyrrhus, as he strives in vain to evade the missiles of his enemies, who surround and attack him (*Andromache* 1135); the joyous dance in which the actual streets of Thebes take part (*Hercules Furens* 782-784); and the dance of dolphins in the sea, led by a ship as "*chorēgus*" (*Helen* 1451-1456).

Two plays of Euripides, by virtue of their exceptional character, challenge a closer examination for possible variations from the norm in the matter of the dancing. These are the *Alcestis* and the *Bacchae*.

The *Alcestis*, staged in 438 B.C., is usually regarded as something of an experiment. Shorter than usual, the play was produced as the last of a group of four plays presented by Euripides at the City Dionysia. It takes the place of the customary satyr play—but it is definitely not a satyr play, nor a comedy. For this reason, some scholars treat the *Alcestis* apart from the author's tragedies. However, a survey of the dances and dance gestures indicated reveals no essential differences in these respects from other plays by the same author. There is a continuing opportunity for mourning gestures throughout the major part of the play. In lines 252-257 we find the common mention of oars and rowing—this time with reference to Charon's boat. One choral ode (568-605) furnishes some relief from the pathos of the play, in its reminiscence of Apollo's sojourn at the court of Admetus, in earlier days. It contains an interesting passage (578-585) in which mention is made of how, when Apollo served as herdsman to Admetus, "spotted lynxes," a "dapple-skinned fawn," and even a "blood-flecked band of lions" came stepping from the woods as Apollo played his lyre, and danced lightly to his music! Whether the chorus here actually danced a few steps of a light nature, we can only surmise. At line 1155, after the miraculous return of Alcestis from the dead, Admetus bids the people celebrate with dances and offerings to the gods, but there is no indication that the chorus here begins the happy dances. At the end of the play, the chorus marches out on five lines (1159-1163), praising the gods for the marvel that they have seen.

The *Bacchae* is spectacularly different from the *Alcestis*—and from any other tragedy which has come down to us. Into it Euripides has breathed the very breath of the barbarous rites in honor of the fertility deity Dionysus—the hysterical dance mania of women worshippers which swept over much of Asia Minor, the islands, and ultimately Greece as well, in pre-classical times, even as a similar dance mania of women raged over Western Europe in the Middle Ages.[66]

The play begins with a prologue (1-63) in which Dionysus, returning from Lydia, Phrygia, Persia, Bactria, Arabia, and the coast of Asia Minor, comes to his native Thebes. He boasts that his ritual dances have spread over all these lands; and he further boasts of how he has now maddened the women of Thebes because they denied his divine birth—driving them to hysterical "mountain dances" against their will. He threatens still more terrible vengeance, now that Pentheus, the new king, has banned his frenzied worship from Thebes. He then calls to the chorus, Asiatic Bacchanals who have followed him to Greece. He bids them strike their Phrygian hand-drums—*tympana*—and dance madly until

---

[66] E. R. Dodds, *Euripides—The Bacchae* (Oxford, 1960), pp. xiv, xvi; Lawler, "Maenads" (above, note 42), 69-112; also "Dance Mania in Prehistoric Greece," *Classical Outlook*, XXIV (1947), 38-39.

the whole city will come out to see them. Dionysus himself goes off to lead the dances of other Bacchanals in the glens of Mount Cithaeron.

The *parodos* (64-169) must have been dramatically effective. Singing a hymn to Dionysus, the members of the chorus burst in. They order unbelievers out of their path. They speak of mountain-dancing, of the shaking of the *thyrsus*, of serpents twining in their hair, of the wearing of the fawn-skin. They associate their dance with that of the Curetes and the Corybantes, and of the satyrs as well. They liken themselves to frisking colts. They beat *tympana*, and play on flutes. They shriek wildly. They tell of the joy of dancing until they faint, of tearing and eating the flesh and drinking the blood of a goat. Apparently they accompany their words with a dance imitative of all the characteristic phases of the savage ritual which they describe, and they may indeed finish in a fainting pose.

Many editors have noted the way in which the meters of the choral passages in the *Bacchae*, and especially those in the *parodos*, enhance the effect of the play. E. R. Dodds,[67] in particular, emphasizes the use of the ionic *a minore*, especially in the *parodos*, and conjectures (p. 72) that "its use was doubtless traditional for Dionysiac plays." He notes also that "the excited and swiftly changing rhythms seem to reflect the Dionysiac unrest" (p. 73).

In the ensuing episode (170-369) Cadmus and Teiresias, both old men, appear in Dionysiac garb and declare their intention of obeying the power of the god and joining in his ritual dances. Pentheus, the king, upbraids them for succumbing to the Dionysiac hysteria, and threatens to fetter all who take part in the rites. The choral ode which follows (370-433) is calmer than the *parodos*, but still contains some ecstatic apostrophizing of Dionysus, and continuing emphasis upon the importance of the dance in his worship. Dionysus is now captured and brought in, and Pentheus has him carried off to prison.

The next choral ode (519-575) is again a Dionysiac hymn, this time dignified in tone; and following immediately upon it Dionysus, who has freed himself of his chains, enters and inspires the chorus to sing and dance once more. The Bacchantes fall to the

---

[67] Dodds (above, note 66), pp. 72-74.

ground as they see the earthquake and fire which Dionysus has called forth to destroy the palace of the king.

In a passage of stupendous power a messenger now reports to Pentheus (660-774) details of the crazed dance of the snake-crowned Bacchantes on Cithaeron, with the king's mother, Agave, as leader of one of the three participating bands of women. The women are called "swift hounds" (731) and likened to flying birds (748-749). They tear animals to pieces (735-747), and chase men off with their *thyrsi* (762-764). This speech would, of course, serve as a body of "stage directions" for the dances actually performed by the chorus at various other points in the play.

Pentheus, angered, determines to subdue the Bacchic frenzy by force, but Dionysus, whom he does not recognize, persuades him to put on the garb of a Bacchant to spy on the women. The ensuing choral ode (862-911) once more treats of Dionysiac dances—and could be accompanied by them. The latter part of the ode emphasizes solemnly the fact that mortals must follow the law of the gods.

In an episode almost grimly humorous, Pentheus now comes in, already under the influence of Dionysiac frenzy, and wearing the garb of a Bacchant. Dionysus helps him adjust his costume. After they depart, a choral ode (977-1023), again filled with vivid references to the revels of the Bacchantes, foretells the slaying of Pentheus. The prediction is immediately confirmed by a messenger. The ensuing brief choral ode (1153-1164) begins with an exhortation to a joyous dance, specifically named a *kallinikos* (1161). After the dance the mood changes to one of horror, as Agave is seen approaching.

There follows the powerful episode in which the crazed Agave, mother of Pentheus, bearing her dead son's head on her staff, and believing that she has slain an animal, exults wildly. Her performance would border on dancing, and some scholars have, indeed, called hers the greatest "dancing role" in Greek tragedy. The chorus would, of course, reflect in gestures a strong emotional reaction to her words. Then, under the questioning of her father, Cadmus, Agave regains her reason and lapses into bitter grief over her terrible deed. Dionysus, appearing, decrees exile for both Agave and Cadmus, and makes it clear that the whole tragedy has been caused by the resistance of mortals to the power of the

[55]

gods. The chorus goes out quietly, marveling upon what it has seen (1388-1392).

Euripides' purpose in setting forth so sensationally in Dionysus' theatre in Athens the horrors of his primitive worship is not clear, although there has been much speculation on the subject. Dodds[68] points out that even in Euripides' day—and indeed down into the second Christian century—ritual mountain dances, performed at night by women devotees of Dionysus, could actually be seen in Delphi and elsewhere. At any rate, Euripides succeeded in presenting a play filled with "pity and terror," and abounding in opportunities for the staging of spectacular dances.

The concluding lines of the *Wasps* of Aristophanes (1474-1537), although they are part of a comedy, are important for a study of the dance of tragedy. As a matter of fact, they are of considerable general importance as well, for they form the only surviving example of what might be called an actual description of a dance of the Greek theatre of the best period.

In this passage Xanthias reports that Philocleon, having drunk more wine than is good for him, has started to dance "those old dances with which Thespis used to contend for a prize" (1479), and appears to be going to keep on dancing all night (1478). He has even challenged contemporary tragic dancers to a competition with him (1480-1481). Just before Philocleon comes out of his house, he demands that the bolts be undone (1484), for, as he says, "that is the beginning of the *schēma*"—i.e., of the dance (1484-1485). This is oddly reminiscent of the dance figure and the flute music variously called *thyrokopikon* and *krousithyron*, "knocking at the door."[69] Next Philocleon (1487-1489) describes, and presumably executes, a figure with strong contortion of the ribs and vertebrae, and with much snorting—a figure which suggests the *poiphygma*, a snorting, roaring, terrifying *schēma*, with accompanying lunges at the audience, probably used most often in animal dances.[70] Claiming Phrynichus as his model, Philocleon

---

[68] Dodds (above, note 66), pp. xiii, xiv, xvi and *passim;* also "Maenadism in the *Bacchae*," *Harvard Theological Review*, XXXIII (1940), 155-176; Gilbert Norwood, *The Riddle of the Bacchae* (Manchester, 1908); Plutarch *De prim. frig.* 18.953 D; *Alex.* 2.5-6.

[69] Athenaeus 14.618 C; cf. Aeschylus *Choephorae* 652-656.

[70] Hesychius *s.v.* "poiphygma"; Johannes Meursius, "*Orchestra*," in Jacobus Gronovius' *Thesaurus Grecarum Antiquitatum* (Venice, 1732-1737),

now (1490) crouches, imitating a fighting cock, and then (1492) kicks his leg "up to heaven." He does this with so much gusto that Xanthias (or the chorus) anxiously bids him to "look out for himself" (1493). Next Philocleon (1494-1495) whirls his joints in their sockets, in a way which Bdelycleon pronounces sheer madness (1496).

And now (1497-1499) Philocleon challenges contemporary tragic dancers again, and one of the sons of Carcinus appears. Carcinus was a tragic poet of Aristophanes' day whose sons were also playwrights, and are said to have been dancers as well. Philocleon scornfully threatens to swallow up the newcomer (1502), and to "destroy him with an *emmeleia* of the knuckles" (1503). The other sons of Carcinus enter, and are greeted with similar insults. Beginning with line 1516, the chorus withdraws a little, so that the dancers may perform freely—as they proceed to do. The chorus details their antics: the dancers spin like tops (1517), leap high as do shrimps on the sand (1519-1521), swing one foot in a circle (1524), and kick high into the air, after the manner of Phrynichus (1525). A scholiast on line 1524 says that the word used here, *Phrynicheion*, denoting a high kick, was actually the name of a *schēma* of the tragic dance;[71] however, he may be making the statement on the authority of this very passage.

The dancers whirl, step around in a circular path, and strike their abdomens (1529), then kick "up to heaven" again, and once more imitate spinning tops (1530). In line 1531 the chorus informs us that Carcinus himself creeps in *(proserpei)*, in admiration for his sons. Finally (1536-1537) the *choreutae* bid the other dancers lead them out; they say that never before has anyone led a comic chorus out dancing.

This famous passage has perplexed and challenged students of the drama and the dance from the days of the scholiasts to the present. In the main, four theories as to the nature of this particular dance have been advanced: (1) that it does portray the dances used by Thespis and other early playwrights; (2) that it is a burlesque of new dances used in the tragedy of Aristophanes'

VIII, *s.v.* "poiphygma"; Lillian B. Lawler, *"Orchēsis Phobera,"* American *Journal of Philology*, LXVII (1936), 67-70.

[71] Roos (above, note 39), p. 132, takes issue with this, and believes the use of the word in this manner is a joke.

day; (3) that it is the *sikinnis,* the characteristic dance of the satyr play; (4) that it is really the *kordax,* the distinctive dance of comedy. Most recently the passage has been the subject of a thorough-going study by Ervin Roos, a Swedish scholar,[72] who has come to the conclusion that Aristophanes is not portraying a dance of the theatre at all, but, in order to show the low point to which some of the tragic dances of his day have fallen, here brings into the Dionysiac theatre the wanton dances of courtesans, which were often imitated by drunken youths in the streets of the city. The performance, Roos says, is made still more repugnant by the fact that it is led by a stiff, clumsy, ugly old man.

The problem will in all probability never be solved to the satisfaction of all scholars in the field. From the nature of the *schēmata* described in the passage, I am inclined to agree with those scholars who believe that Aristophanes here makes use of elements of the *kordax* in a highly exaggerated burlesque of various new and free dances and figures with which tragic and other writers of the day were experimenting. A scholiast on *Clouds* 542 says that Aristophanes used the *kordax* in the *Wasps;* presumably he means this passage, but he does not say so. It should be pointed out that the *kordax* and the dances of courtesans are in origin and in essence the same thing—stimulating or fertility dances, examples of which are found from primitive times in the ritual of many nature deities, of whom Dionysus, presiding divinity of the drama, was one. The *kordax* itself was performed in the cult of Artemis, who was a goddess of fertility.[73] I do not think we can take the passage in the *Wasps* seriously as a picture of the dance in Greek tragedy, new or old.

All of this brings us to the frequently-posed question as to just what, precisely, the *emmeleia* was. Was it merely the formal, tetragonal, march-like performance attested for the chorus of tragedy? Or could it at times be free, reflecting with varied choreography actual dances performed in Greek communities? Is it always a choral dance, as the Suidas *Lexicon* states *(s.v.),* or could it be performed by a single dancer?[74] Is the term restricted to *some*

---

[72] Roos (above, note 39).

[73] Pausanias 6.22.1.

[74] Roos (above, note 39), *passim,* devotes much attention to the *emmeleia.* Cf. especially his pages 143, 155-156, and 161-162. He believes that it was

of the dances in the plays, and if so, to which dances? Or does it include all the rich, colorful dances in the plays, in choral odes and elsewhere? Can it be applied also to dignified dances *outside* of tragedy?

Unfortunately, we have from antiquity no clear definition of the *emmeleia*, nor have we in Greek art, so far as we can determine, any representation of the *emmeleia*. That the term is not always too narrow in its application is indicated by the comment in the Suidas *Lexicon (s.v.)* that the *emmeleia* includes "dancing with song and dancing in accompaniment to spoken words." Plato's brief treatment of the subject[75] apparently equates the *emmeleia* with all dances which are "peaceful" (as distinct from "warlike" dances such as the pyrrhic) and are at the same time "temperate," "earnest" *(spoudaiai)*, and "beautiful" *(kalai)*, displaying "solemn, stately" movements *(epi to semnon)* of "handsome" bodies and "noble" *(gennaiōn)* souls. He classes as *emmeleiai* the dances performed to the gods, especially dances offered by people who are joyous, prosperous, and thankful. Thus to Plato, at least, *emmeleia* is a generic term for dignified, restrained dances of many varieties, among them the dances used in tragedy of the highest type. To the lexicographers, on the other hand, the *emmeleia* is specifically the dance of tragedy.

It is worthy of note that Plato carefully excludes Bacchic dances from the *emmeleia*, and relegates those dances to non-citizens. This fact is interesting in the light of the Dionysiac associations of tragedy in general, and, in particular, of the use of Dionysiac motifs in choral passages of the *Bacchae* of Euripides.

Our discussion of the dance of the developed Athenian tragedy (and of the dithyramb as well) has been based for the most part upon the performance at one Dionysiac festival alone—the City Dionysia, celebrated in Athens in the month Elaphebolion (March-April). This was the most magnificent of the Attic festivals in honor of Dionysus, the one attended by the greatest number of foreign guests as well as of Athenian citizens. It was featured by competitions in newly written dithyrambs, tragedies,

---

so restrained that even the Greeks themselves hardly considered it to be a real dance.

[75] Plato *Laws* 7.814 E-816 D.

comedies, and satyr plays, and in its performances all these genres reached their highest development.

There were, however, other festivals to Dionysus at which dramatic performances of varied types were featured. The Lenaea, celebrated in the month Gamelion (January-February), attracted a goodly number of Athenians, but few foreigners—probably in large part because of the weather. At the Lenaea there were competitions in tragedy and in comedy, but comedy was definitely favored over tragedy—and in fact it is possible that at this festival the comic performances actually antedated the tragic competitions. There were no dithyrambic contests. Some scholars believe that younger poets may have found it easier to gain a hearing at the Lenaea than at the City Dionysia.

In the month of Poseideon (December), rural Dionysia were celebrated in communities in the neighborhood of Athens, the one at the harbor-town of Piraeus being outstanding. At these festivals tragedies and comedies were presented; however, it is believed that the plays there were usually not new, but were rather dramas which had already won competitions in Athens proper, either recently or at some earlier date.

At all these lesser festivals the dances which formed a part of the performances, although a little less sumptuously costumed and staged, a little less skillfully performed and directed, yet must have been of essentially the same type as those to be seen at the great City Dionysia.

Beginning in the fourth century B.C., changes appeared in the dramatic performances. From about the middle of that century on, tragedies written in former years, particularly those by the three great writers of tragedy, were re-produced. On one occasion, for example (in the year 341/340), the dramatic events at the City Dionysia began with a single satyr play, then proceeded to a tragedy by Euripides, and then went on to a tragic competition in which playwrights of the day presented a trilogy each. Later, the dramatists at the City Dionysia customarily presented two new tragedies each. Not until the end of the first century of the Christian era was the presentation of new tragedies at the City Dionysia discontinued; and even after that the re-production of tragedies by earlier masters went on for a considerable time.

There were undoubtedly many alterations in the dance of

[60]

tragedy in the late classical period. One change seems to have been the introduction of mute "supernumeraries" into the chorus. We are told that even before that innovation was made, the tragic poet Agathon, who lived in the latter half of the fifth century, had begun the use of *embolima*[76]—choral songs, with dance, which were not connected with the plot of the play, but were merely inserted as interludes, and could be used as well in one play as in another. Other playwrights, including perhaps Euripides, followed Agathon in the use of *embolima*. (Cf. *Iph. Taur.* 1234-1282.) In time the interludes seem to have been reduced to mere dances, without song. Also, there must have been changes in the dance necessitated by such developments as, for example, the gradual reduction in the size and importance of the tragic chorus, and the use of newer musical instruments to accompany the dance of tragedy. Changes in the structure of the theatre, too, had their effect. With the transfer of all the action to a stage in the Greco-Roman period, the old "tetragonal" evolutions of the chorus, and other large dance formations, so impressive in the great "dancing-place" of the classical theatre, would, of course, be out of the question. Many scholars[77] believe that by the middle of the second century B.C. all choral dancing had ceased in tragedy, and that the choral odes were then sung without dancing. This is borne out by a passage in Philodemus,[78] who quotes the second-century philosopher Diogenes of Babylon as saying sadly that since the dance has now disappeared entirely from the drama, there is nothing in the plays that contributes anything to "the beautiful and the noble."

In the third century B.C. actors' and musicians' guilds had been organized. The artists were held in high esteem, and were given special privileges. Many actors became also producers, and exercised a great deal of freedom in adapting famous plays of earlier periods (and presumably their dances as well) to their own needs. New dramatic and musical contests were established, and many new theatres were built, to which the artists traveled, all through the Greek lands. We have no mention of dancing in these contests.

---

[76] Aristotle *Poetics* 1456 A, 29-30; cf. Gerald F. Else, *Aristotle's Poetics: The Argument* (Cambridge, Mass., 1957), pp. 552-557.

[77] Cf. A. W. Pickard-Cambridge, *The Theatre of Dionysus at Athens* (Oxford, 1946), p. 195.

[78] *De musica* 4.7.1-8, p. 70 Kemke.

However, in the Greco-Roman period, beginning in the Augustan Age, there is some resurgence of the tragic dance in the performance of the *pantomimus*. The pantomimic dance, said to have been "invented" by Pylades and Bathyllus, reduced the plots of Greek tragedy and mythology to elaborate, rhythmic dumb show.[79] For each performance there was usually but one actor-dancer, who took all the principal roles in turn, with the aid of several masks and sumptuous costumes. To accompany his dance-portrayal there was an orchestra composed of lyres, Pan-pipes, cymbals, *tympana*, Egyptian *sistra* or metal rattles, and the wood-and-iron percussion instrument operated by the foot, and called the *scabellum*. In the intervals between the episodes, while the *pantomimus* changed his costume, an off-stage choir sang appropriate lyrics. Performances of this type became incredibly popular—even to the point of precipitating street fights between partisans of rival dancers—and they ultimately superseded tragedy as a dramatic form. The exhibitions of the *pantomimi* continued at least until the end of the fourth century in the West, and, in the East, until the sixth century, when they were banned by the emperor Justinian.

---

[79] Vincenzo Rotolo, *Il Pantomimo* (Palermo, 1957); Lillian B. Lawler, "Portrait of a Dancer," *Classical Journal*, XLI (1946), 241-247.

III

THE DANCE
OF COMEDY

In Greece, comedy as a literary form developed later than did tragedy, although many of the primitive performances and rituals from which comedy ultimately evolved must have been of great antiquity.[1]

We are probably not aware of all the elements which combined to create Athenian comedy. Aristotle says (*Poet.* 1449 A, 38-B, 5) that the origins of comedy are unknown to him, since comedy was not regarded highly for some time after it had its beginning. However, he seems to believe (*Poet.* 1449 A, 9-14) that it had its origin in the improvisations of the leaders of phallic or fertility processions held in various Greek cities,[2] and he notes (1448 A, 29-38;

---

[1] For the origin and development of Greek comedy see the general works listed in note 1 to Chapter I, and also the following: A. W. Pickard-Cambridge, *The Theatre of Dionysus at Athens* (Oxford, 1946); also, *The Dramatic Festivals of Athens* (Oxford, 1953); John W. White, *The Verse of Greek Comedy* (London, 1912); Hans Herter, *Vom Dionysischen Tanz zum komischen Spiel* (Iserlohn, 1947); Luigi M. Catteruccia, *Pitture vascolari italiote di soggetto teatrale comico* (Rome, 1951); Heinz Schnabel, *Kordax* (Munich, 1910); Ervin Roos, *Die tragische Orchestik im Zerrbild der altattischen Komödie* (Lund, 1951); K. J. Maidment, "The Later Comic Chorus," *Classical Quarterly*, XXIX (1935), 1-24; E. Capps, "The Chorus in the Later Greek Drama," *American Journal of Archaeology*, Ser. I, X (1895), 287-325; C. T. Murphy, "A Survey of Recent Work on Aristophanes and Old Comedy," *Classical Weekly*, XL (1956), 201-211.

[2] But cf. Gerald F. Else, *Aristotle's Poetics: The Argument* (Cambridge, Mass., 1957), pp. 135-163. Also, some scholars, e.g. Francis M. Cornford, in *The Origin of Attic Comedy* (London, 1914), have held that Greek comedy originated in a primitive fertility drama involving processions, a sacrifice, a feast, a combat, death and resurrection, and a "sacred marriage." Other

B, 1-3), without taking a stand on the question, that the Dorians claimed the "invention" of comedy as well as tragedy.

The processions which Aristotle had in mind were engaged in by volunteer singers who hoped by their activities to invoke the powers of fertility for the community, and to drive away evil. The marchers, crowned with flowers and ivy, carried large phallic symbols on poles, and sang hymns to the nature god Dionysus. In some of the processions the participants wore masks, in others they did not. Some of the performances were characterized by witty but abusive and obscene comments made by the marchers to various members of the crowd of onlookers—who then retorted in kind, and spiritedly, thereby inducing a quarrel or contest. The song featuring personal abuse and invective is well-known magic among primitive peoples, even today, for the expulsion of evil spirits. A general idea of the processions may be obtained from Aristophanes' *Acharnians* 237-279.

But the phallic processions were not the only forerunners of Athenian comedy. Vintage revels seem to have had a part in its development (cf. Athenaeus 2.40 A-B; Plutarch *De Proverb. Alex.* 30), as did *kōmoi*, or "revel dances." The word *kōmoidia*, "comedy," is indeed derived from the word *kōmos*.

The *kōmoi* were of various sorts. In one, frequently portrayed on vase paintings, young men, feeling exuberantly happy after a drinking bout, rollicked through the town, singing uproariously, kicking up their heels in impromptu dances, scuffling, and playing practical jokes upon one another and upon luckless passersby. *Kōmoi* of this sort often took place at night, by torch-light. Sometimes they followed wedding processions.[3]

Another form of the *kōmos* was more sedate; in it a group of men marched through the town to the accompaniment of a flute-player, stopping now and then to sing and dance. Sometimes the procession honored Dionysus, or another god, or a mythological

---

theories will be found in A. W. Pickard-Cambridge's *Dithyramb, Tragedy, and Comedy* (1st ed.; Oxford, 1927), pp. 104-107; (2nd ed.; Oxford, 1962), pp. 132-187.

[3] *Kōmoi* of the first type are referred to in Pollux 4.99; Hesiod *Scut.* 281; Homeric *Hymn to Hermes* 481; Euripides *Alcestis* 918 and *Cyclops* 534-538; Aristophanes *Plutus* 1038-1046 and "chorou"; Menander *Dyskolos* 230-232 and "chorou"; *Arbitrants*, close of first act and "chorou"; Philostratus *Imag.* 1.3.5; Athenaeus 8.348 C.

character (cf. Euripides, *Bacchae* 1168; *Helen* 1468-1475; *Cyclops* 37-40). On other occasions the participants escorted an athletic victor or a poet or a prominent citizen to his home. This is the *kōmos* referred to in the choral lyrics of Pindar and Bacchylides (cf. *Olymp.* 8.10; 11.16; 14.22; *Pyth.* 3.73; 5.22; *Nem.* 3.5; 9.50; *Isth.* 2.31; 3.8; 8.4, etc.; Bacchylides 10.12-13). By extension, the word in this sense is sometimes applied to the dithyrambic choruses.

Occasionally we hear of *kōmoi* the participants in which were men garbed as women, and women garbed as men. These seem to go back to early fertility rituals and dances, such as those of the Dorian *bryllachistai* (Hesychius *s.vv.*, "brydalicha," "bryllachistai"; Pollux 4.104), who sought by the transvestism to outwit evil spirits.

Still a different version of the *kōmos* may be seen in the various animal dances and processions which were popular among all the Greeks throughout their history. Such mummery had a place in many cults, notably in that of Artemis as nature and fertility goddess, and perhaps also in that of Dionysus (the two cults had many elements in common). A scholiast on Theocritus[4] tells us of a rustic *kōmos* at Syracuse in honor of Artemis Lyaia, in which singers and dancers wearing "stags' horns on their heads" carried skins of wine and huge loaves of bread stamped with the figures of animals of various sorts, and took part in a competition (apparently in singing and dancing), the winner in which "took the bread of the loser." Ritual animal mummery, serious at first, usually degenerates into buffoonery; thus early mummery had a tendency to become a "funny" dance, and it seems to have had some place in the evolution of Greek comedy. It is not surprising, then, that when comedy took form as such, the performers frequently appeared in masks and costumes suggesting fantastically-garbed "birds," "dolphins," or animals of one sort or another.[5]

At first there was no hint of plot in any of the processions or dances. The Dorian Greeks, however, had developed, in Greece

---

[4] H. L. Ahrens, *Bucolicorum Graecorum Theocriti Bionis Moschi Reliquiae* (Lipsiae, 1869), II, 5; quoted also in Pickard-Cambridge, *Dithyramb* (above, note 2), 1st ed.; p. 248; 2nd ed.; p. 296; and in Martin P. Nilsson, *Griechische Feste* (Leipzig, 1906), p. 200, n. 1.

[5] A. B. Cook, *Zeus* (Cambridge, 1914-1940), I, 696-705; II, 460-501.

proper and in Italy and Sicily as well, various crude farces in which actors, wearing masks and ludicrous "stuffed" costumes, set forth brief plots, with much obscenity and horseplay. As time advanced, it appears that Attic comedy borrowed from the Dorian farces the idea of actors, plots, and costumes, incorporated them into its performances, and then went on to develop the true genre of comedy.[6]

The Megarians in particular—both those of Megara in Greece and those of Megara Hyblaea in Sicily—claimed to be the originators of comedy. It is true that Epicharmus, from the latter city, did raise the literary quality of the Dorian farce to the status of real comedy early in the fifth century before Christ; but tradition ascribes the "invention" of comic choruses to Susarion, working in Icaria just before the middle of the sixth century. It is generally conjectured that Susarion changed the *kōmos* from a procession through the town to a performance in a "dancing-place," presumably at the Dionysiac festival of the Lenaea. The addition of actors and a plot, and of masks and costumes appropriate to the plot, would have come as a logical sequel to the innovations of Susarion.

Many poets now began to take an interest in comedy. They reduced or eliminated improvisation, improved the plot, and set the number of speaking actors at three, as in tragedy (although later one or two extra actors were added occasionally, for small parts of a few lines each). They incorporated into their plays the popular invective and obscenity of the fertility rituals, and political and personal references as well. The "padded union suit" costume, conspicuous phallus, and grotesque mask of the actor became conventionalized.[7] As in tragedy, all the performers were men, where necessary impersonating women. The chorus was now carefully trained, usually by the poet himself.

The chorus became stabilized at twenty-four *choreutae*—at times separating into hostile semi-choruses, each with a leader or *cory-*

---

[6] This view of the origin of the plot element in Attic comedy is attacked by Hans Herter (above, note 1); but Max Pohlenz, "Die Entstehung der attischen Komödie," *Nachrichten der Akademie der Wissenschaften in Göttingen, Phil.-Hist. Klasse* (1949), 31-44, contradicts Herter and re-affirms the generally accepted theory. Cornford (above, note 2), presents a different hypothesis.

[7] On costumes and masks see Pickard-Cambridge, *Dramatic Festivals* (above, note 1), pp. 175-238.

phaeus, perhaps in reminiscence of the quarrels which often arose between performers and bystanders in connection with the early village processions. Dramatic episodes or scenes were set apart by choral odes, some of them of great beauty. A prologue was added, in the manner of the tragic prologue. The entrance of the chorus was in effect a *parodos,* as in tragedy, and its departure at the end of the play (reminiscent of the processional character of the *kōmos*) was called an *exodos.*

At Athens, informal performances of comedy seem to have been put on by "volunteers" at the Dionysiac festival of the Lenaea, in January-February, beginning at about the middle of the sixth century before Christ. From then on throughout the classical period, comedy was a feature of the Lenaea. At the Rural Dionysia, celebrated in December in towns and villages throughout Attica, comedies were often performed. Many of the plays so produced may have been comedies which had been introduced earlier at Athens.

In spite of its religious associations, there was always a feeling that comedy was a less worthy form of the drama, and it was not until about 501 B.C. that comedy was added to the dramatic events of the City Dionysia. In about 486 B.C. the state finally took over and dignified the comic performances at that festival. In that year winners in a competition in comedy are first recorded, and from then on *chorēgī* are assigned to costume and train the comic choruses.

Athenian comedy down to the beginning of the fourth century is known as Old Comedy. There are said to have been many excellent writers of Old Comedy, but outstanding among them all was Aristophanes. The plays of this period were spectacular, and were enlivened with slapstick and horseplay. Often the plots were fantastically imaginative. The choruses portrayed human beings, animals, cities, islands, clouds, ships, centaurs, sphinxes, and all sorts of allegorical beings, and their elaborate, sometimes weird, costumes and masks added to the general effect. There are, indeed, occasional references to the taking off of cloaks or other portions of the bulky costumes to enable the chorus to dance or move more freely, as there are also in Middle Comedy.[8] There

---

[8] Aristophanes *Acharn.* 627—"But, taking off [our cloaks], let us get

seems to have been in each play a great deal of spirited dancing. Middle Comedy and New Comedy succeeded Old Comedy. These we shall consider later. Meanwhile we may direct our attention to what is known of the dances, orchestic patterns, and dance figures which had a place in the performances of Old Comedy.

The chorus of Old Comedy, like that of tragedy, is said to have been "tetragonal"—i.e., it normally entered and left the *orchēstra* in a solid rectangle. Since it was composed of twenty-four *choreutae*, it could be drawn up in four "ranks" and six "files," or six "ranks" and four "files."[9] As in tragedy, after the prologue the chorus entered on the right of the audience, ideally with the *coryphaeus* and the best dancers on the left side of the rectangular group as it advanced. When all its members were well within the *orchēstra*, it customarily turned to face the spectators, and the line which had been on the left now became the front row. The chorus usually entered marching and singing. In practice, the formal entry was frequently abandoned for a special reason—for a running entrance, as in *Acharnians* 204 and perhaps *Peace* 301, *Knights* 247-254, and *Plutus* 257; for a "flying entrance," as in *Birds* 295-296; or for some irregular or amusing formation to suit the plot of the play, sometimes even with individual entries on the part of the several members of the chorus, as in *Birds* 267-290; *Ecclesiazusae* 30-51, 300; and probably *Thesmophoriazusae* 295. In at least one play, the *Lysistrata*, the half-choruses enter separately, the "men" entering at line 254, the "women" at line 319.

In like manner, the formal marching exit, or *exodos*, could be varied to suit the exigencies of the plot. At times it becomes a victory procession—as in the *Acharnians* and the *Ecclesiazusae*. Sometimes, as in the *Peace* and the *Birds*, the *exodos* becomes a wedding procession.[10] In the *Wasps* the chorus leader orders the sons of Carcinus, who have been engaging in a boisterous dance, to lead out the chorus,[11] and asserts at the same time that never

---

at the anapaests"; *Peace* 729-733; *Thesmo.* 655-656; *Lysis.* 614-615, 637, 662, 685; cf. Athenaeus 10.417 E.

[9] See the discussion of the formation of the chorus of tragedy, above, Chapter II.

[10] Cf. Cornford (above, note 2), pp. 8-34.

[11] *Wasps* 1535-1537; cf. schol. ad loc.

before has anyone (perhaps an actor) led out a comic chorus dancing. The conclusions of these and other plays of Aristophanes will be considered in detail later.

Throughout the body of the play, during the period of Old Comedy, the chorus was of great importance. Sometimes various members of the chorus were personalized, and spoke with the actors. Other lines were sung, or given in recitative. The dancing, too, was important, and varied. As in tragedy, the choral odes were accompanied with dancing, as were portions of the *parabasis*, the direct address of the comic chorus to the audience. Also, orchestic gestures were used to follow and interpret the speech and song of actors and chorus.[12] There were both group and solo dances. Some of the former may have been of the same "tetragonal" marching pattern as that customarily associated with the *parodos*. Some of the latter were assuredly very animated, not to say uproarious, in tone.

All our sources tell us[13] that the characteristic dance of Old Comedy was called the *kordax*. This word seems to have denoted a specific dance—not all the dancing that appeared in comedy. Aristophanes, for example, announced publicly in his *Clouds* (540) that his Muse, in this play, at least, would not use the *kordax*. (However, we are told specifically[14] that he did use it elsewhere.)

Some scholars hold that the *kordax* was always a solo dance. It is indeed performed at times by single dancers.[15] Aristophanes himself (*Clouds* 553-556) mentions it as being performed in the Old Comedy of Eupolis by "a drunken old woman." However, choruses or groups dance it also;[16] probably in a chorus the *choreutae* danced freely, functioning not as a group, but rather as individuals. Schnabel thinks it was performed only by actors, not by the chorus, but Roos has refuted his argument well, and has

---

[12] Athenaeus 1.21 F, 22 A; schol. Aristophanes *Clouds* 1352; cf. Plato *Laws* 7.816 A; *Rep.* 396 A-397 B.

[13] Pollux 4.99; Athenaeus 1.20 E; Aristophanes *Clouds* 540 and schol. ad loc., and also on 555; Demosthenes *Olynth.* 2.18; Theophrastus *Char.* 6.3; Hesychius *s.v.* "kordax"; Suidas *s.v.* "kordakizei"; *Et. Mag.* 635.2, *s.v.* "orchēstai"; Lucian *Salt.* 26.

[14] Schol. *Clouds* 542.

[15] Lucian *Icaromenippus* 27; Petronius *Cena* 52.8.

[16] Theophrastus *Char.* 6.3 and schol. ad loc.; Lucian *Dionys.* 1.

held that it may have been danced by either actors or *choreutae*.[17] It was obviously not the tetragonal march of the chorus.

Ancient writers are unanimous in their testimony that the dance was lascivious, ignoble, obscene. Athenaeus (14.629 D) includes it in a list of dances which he characterizes a little vaguely as "rather definite in form," "rather colorful," and possessing a "somewhat simple choreography," but he, too, in another passage (14.631 D), labels it *phortikos*, "vulgar." Plato (*Laws* 7.816 D-E) would prohibit freeborn citizens from dancing it. Other ancient writers say that when performed by private individuals the *kordax* is a sign of drunkenness and of slack morals, and that decent people never perform it without wearing a mask.[18]

The Greek traveler and author Pausanias (6.22.1) tells us that, at a shrine in Elis, Artemis was designated as "Kordaka," and that in her honor was performed a ritual *kordax*, brought to Elis from Sipylus in Lydia by followers of Pelops. In this connection it is significant that many votive masks made of clay, found in the shrine of Artemis Orthia in Sparta, portray drunken old women. Again, an inscription from Minoa, on the island of Amorgos,[19] attests performances of the *kordax* in honor of the Pythian Apollo. The inscription is a late one (of the second century of the Christian era), but ritual is notably conservative, and the dances may well have been of great antiquity. Both Apollo and Artemis, as we know, were worshipped, especially in the pre-classical period, as divinities of animal fertility. The worship of Artemis, in particular, was much influenced by the cults of pre-Greek and Asiatic mother-goddesses in which lewd and orgiastic dances were by no means uncommon. Presumably in the cults of Apollo and Artemis the ritualistic performances of the *kordax* would be given by trained temple dancers.

Some scholars, notably Schnabel,[20] have expressed the conviction that the origin of the dance of comedy is to be found in the

---

[17] Schnabel (above, note 1), p. 15, refuted by Roos (above, note 1), pp. 153-160.

[18] See above, note 16; cf. Mnesimachus frag. 4.

[19] IG XII¹, p. 246; the text appears also in Lewis R. Farnell's *Cults of the Greek States* (Oxford, 1896-1909), IV, 397, n. 162.

[20] Schnabel (above, note 1), *passim*; but cf. Pickard-Cambridge, *Dithyramb* (1st ed.; above, note 2), pp. 254-266; (2nd ed.; above, note 2), pp. 163-169.

THE DANCE OF COMEDY

worship of the primitive Artemis in the Peloponnesus, and that the dance passed from that cult into the cult of Dionysus. They see performers of some of the Peloponnesian dances in the numerous grotesquely padded, "over-stuffed" figures portrayed in early vase paintings, as well as in various phallic figures in Greek ceramic art. However, the dancers to Artemis are predominantly female, those of the theatrical *kordax* predominantly male—as are those on the vase paintings. It is possible that not one, but several forms of fertility dance are to be seen as the ancestors of the *kordax* in the theatre. As Pickard-Cambridge says,[21] "there was more than one kind of vulgar dance."

The essential nature of the *kordax* is stated concisely by an unknown commentator on Aristophanes' *Clouds* 540: it was a lewd rotation of the abdomen and buttocks. The same rotation, alternating with leaping, is attested by Autocrates[22] for the ritual dances of Lydian maidens in honor of the Ephesian Artemis.

Several *schēmata*, or figures, of the *kordax* are recorded. The most distinctive of these, the one called variously *rhiknousthai*[23] or *diarrhiknousthai*,[24] is given practically the same definition as that given to the *kordax* itself—a lascivious rotation of the thighs, with the body bent far forward.

Along with this figure Pollux (4.99) mentions the *xiphismos*, or "sword thrust." Cratinus (frag. 219, Kock) similarly has *xiphize kai (s)podize kai diarrhiknou*. The *xiphismos* seems to have been originally a figure of the tragic dance which acquired an obscene significance and came into the dance of comedy.[25] In its original significance of a sword thrust it could have been used in such choral passages as that in *Lysistrata* 632-635.

Pollux mentions in the same sentence a figure called the *podismos*. Cratinus has the verb *podize*, as we have just seen. The verb

---

[21] Pickard-Cambridge, *Dithyramb* (1st ed.; above, note 2), p. 260.
[22] Frag. 1, Kock; quoted in Schnabel (above, note 1), p. 42, n. 1. Schnabel illustrates some of the representations in Greek art which have been associated by various scholars with this aspect of the *kordax*.
[23] Photius *s.v.*; Lexiphanes 8; Suidas *s.v.*
[24] Pollux 4.99; Cratinus, frag. 219, Kock; Hesychius *s.vv.* "diariknousthai" (*sic*), "dieriknounto"; *Et. Mag. s.v.* "diarrhiknousthai."
[25] Photius *s.v.* "xiphismos"; Hesychius *s.vv.* "xiphizein" and "xiphismos"; *Et. Mag. s.v.* "xiphismata." See also the discussion of this *schēma* above, in Chapter II.

[71]

means "bind or tie the feet." The *schēma* seems to have been a hop, with both feet held closely together as if tied, and with the body bent forward. We note here, of course, a resemblance to *rhiknousthai, diarrhiknousthai;* and Cratinus has *diarrhiknou* along with *podize.* Scaliger[26] says the figure is one in which "with feet joined, with much effort, they imitated woodpeckers"—"iunctis pedibus, labore plurimo, et conatu picos imitabantur." It may be that one element in the development of the *podismos* was a dance imitative of a hopping bird. In the *Lexicon* of Hesychius *(s.v.)* there is mention of a form of dance "or a leap" called the *diapodismos;* this would seem to be a variant of the *podismos,* as *diarrhiknousthai* is of *rhiknousthai.* On the other hand, the *schēma* known as the *dipodismos,* listed by Athenaeus (14.630 A) with various figures which we have treated above as *schēmata* of the tragic dance, seems to have been originally a "two-foot" dance of some sort, perhaps with lively kicks of one leg and then the other, as in the dance at the end of the *Wasps* (1482-1537); it may later have fused with the *diapodismos.*[27]

Several other dances or *schēmata* which are merely variations of *rhiknousthai* are attested. The *maktēr* or *maktrismos,*[28] listed by Athenaeus as "humorous," and sometimes performed by women of low repute, derived its name from *maktra,* a "kneading trough"— but it was not, as some writers have stated naively, a folk-dance using "work rhythms"![29] It is specifically defined and described by Pollux (4.101) in terms which leave no doubt of its identity with *rhiknousthai.* Its movements obviously reminded the Greeks of a stirring motion. We may here compare the passage in the *Metamorphoses* of Apuleius (2.7), in which the girl Fotis, stirring a pot on the fire, and attracting a young man's attention at the same time, sways her shoulders and hips rhythmically. Similar is the *igdē, igdis, igdisma,*[30] named from *igdē,* "a mortar," *igdizō,*

---

[26] Julius Caesar Scaliger, "De Comoedia et Tragoedia," in Jacobus Gronovius' *Thesaurus Graecarum Antiquitatum* (Venice, 1732-1737), VIII, 1525 F-1526 A.

[27] Cf. Lillian B. Lawler, *"Diplē, Dipodia, Dipodismos," Transactions of the American Philological Association,* LXXVI (1945), 59-73.

[28] Hesychius *s.v.* "maktēr"; Athenaeus 14.629 C and F; Pollux 4.101.

[29] Cf. Schnabel (above, note 1), pp. 7-8 and n. 1.

[30] Pollux 4.101; 10.103-104; Athenaeus 14.629 F; *Et. Mag.* 464.49-52, *s.v.* "igdē"; Suidas *s.v.* "igdisma"; Lillian B. Lawler, "A Mortar Dance," *Classical Journal,* XLIII (1947), 34.

"grind, pound." It was characterized by rotation of the hips, with an occasional sharp jerk of the body, suggestive of the stirring and pounding of a pestle. The Greek word is oddly parallel to the English "grinds" and "bumps," used of the dances of the modern burlesque theatre! To this group of figures and dances is probably to be assigned also the *dritē* or *droitē*, "the vat" or "the kneading trough."[31] Often coupled with the *igdisma* is the figure called variously *lygisma, lygismos, lygistikon, lygizein*[32]—"writhing, twisting, as a willow wand." Philocleon makes use of it in *Wasps* 1487. Also, closely associated with the *maktrismos*, and, indeed, given as variants of it, are the *apokinos* [33] and the *aposeisis*,[34] both of which use a lewd rotation of the hips. The *apokinos* is mentioned in humorous metaphor in Aristophanes' *Knights* 20, by a slave hoping to escape from his master—"find some *apokinos*" (i.e., some means of wriggling away) "from our master." A commentator on the passage (Schol. Ven.) defines the *apokinos* as a vulgar dance, and a song to accompany it; he equates it with the *baukismos*, which we shall consider presently.

The characteristic adjective applied to dancers of these and similar figures, and also to the dancing itself, is *hygros*, "fluid"— reminiscent of our "slippery as an eel." Nor is the modern figure of speech lacking in aptness. There is more than a little evidence that some of the "wriggling" figures of the *kordax* may actually have had a resemblance to various dances in which the dancer writhed in imitation of a snake or a lizard. In connection with the figures we have been noting, some ancient writers mention the *kal(l)abis, kal(l)abides, kal(l)abidia*.[35] In this figure the dancer stepped affectedly and indulged in rotation of the hips. The name of the figure has been connected etymologically with words de-

---

[31] Hesychius *s.v.* "dritē," universally emended to "droitē"; cf. Lillian B. Lawler, "Ladles, Tubs, and the Greek Dance," *American Journal of Philology*, LXXI (1950), 70-72.

[32] Philostratus *Vit. Apoll.* 4.21; Suidas *s.v.* "igdisma"; *Et. Mag.* 464, *s.v.* "igdē." For a different interpretation of the *lygisma* and of the mortar dances, see Roos (above, note 1), pp. 21-75.

[33] Athenaeus 14.629 C and F; Pollux 4.101 and 10.103; Suidas *s.v.* "apokinos."

[34] Pollux 4.101 and 10.103.

[35] Athenaeus 14.629 F, 630 A; Hesychius *s.v.* "kalabis"; Photius *s.v.* "kalabides."

THE DANCE OF THE ANCIENT GREEK THEATRE

noting "lizard,"[36] and has been associated with the figure *proskin-klizein*—"to flick the tail," as a lizard.[37] As a matter of fact, some scholars believe that the pre-Greek root **kal, *skal* may have an association with snakes or lizards; cf. Greek *kalōs*, "rope."[38] In any case, dances in which the dancer contorts his body in imitation of a snake are by no means uncommon, even among primitive peoples today. Ritual dances and songs called *kallabidia, kalaboidia*, or *kalaboutai* formed a part of the ritual of Artemis Dereatis on Mount Taygetus.[39] These were probably similar to the performances of the *kordax* to Artemis Kordaka in Elis. The figure called the *kallibas* or *kallibantes*, although not connected etymologically with the *kalabides*, and denoting simply "walking prettily" (i.e., mincing affectedly), seems to have been of the same general type as the *kalabides*.[40] So, apparently, was the *baukismos*, described in the *Lexicon* of Hesychius (*s.v.*) as an Ionic dance, and by Pollux (4.100) as a *kōmos* in which the dancer steps delicately and "makes his body fluid." The *Lexicon* of Hesychius further defines *baukizesthai* (*s.v.*) as *thryptesthai*, " be wanton," and *baukismata* (*s.v.*) as *trypherōtata*, "very voluptuous" figures. A scholiast on Aristophanes' *Knights* 20 defines the *apokinos* as *baukismos*. Still other figures involving an affected, effeminate walk, with voluptuous hip movements, are those called *saula bainein* or *sauloumenos, diasauloumenos, sauloprōktian, diasalakōnizō, salakōnizō, salakōneuō*.[41] Most of these contain the word *saulos*, which is related etymologically to *sauros*, "lizard,"[42] and imply "flick the tail," as a lizard. Anacreon[43] speaks of the Bassarides, wild female dancers to Dionysus, as *saulai*. The *Lexi-*

---

36 Cf. Hesychius *s.v.* "kalabōtēs."

37 Kurt Latte, *De Saltationibus Graecorum Capita Quinque* (Giessen, 1913), pp. 23-26; on the other hand, some writers have associated the "tail-flicking" figure with dancers costumed as long-tailed *sileni*. Cf. the Autocrates fragment cited above (note 22).

38 Cook (above, note 5), I, 725-726; II, 1087.

39 Hesychius *s.v.* "kalaboidia."

40 Hesychius *s.v.* "kallibantes."

41 Euripides *Cyclops* 40; Aristophanes, frag. 624 Kock; *Wasps* 1169-1173; schol. *Wasps* 1169 and 1173; *Et. Mag. s.v.* "diasauloumenos"; cf. Hesychius *s.v.* "diasauloumenon."

42 Émile Boisacq, *Dictionnaire étymologique de la langue grecque* (Heidelberg, 1950), *s.v.* "saulos."

43 Frag. 55, Bergk.

con of Hesychius defines *saula (s.v.)* as "nimble, soft, voluptuous" —*koupha, hēsycha, tryphera.* This recalls the *kouphikon tropon,* "the nimble manner," listed in the Hesychius *Lexicon (s.v.),* which may also be a figure of the *kordax.*

Additional light may be shed upon some of the writhing *schē-mata* by the dance or *schēma* known as the *mothōn*—which, indeed, may have been used as a part of the *kordax.* Photius *(s.v.)* says it is lewd and *kordax*-like—*kordakōdes;* and the dance actually figures, although perhaps metaphorically, in Aristophanes' *Knights* 697, where a character says, "I have danced the *mothōn*" —[for joy]. The scholiast on that line, and also Pollux (4.101), emphasizes the lewdness of the dance; Pollux adds that it is *nauti-kon*—apparently "performed by sailors." Athenaeus (14.618 C) mentions the *mothōn* as a kind of flute music regularly accompanied with dancing. In Aristophanes' *Knights* 635 the word is used as the name of a sort of "goblin" of drunkenness and wantonness. The word is used to mean a "rogue" in Aristophanes' *Plutus* 279; a scholiast on the passage says that *mothōn* also denotes a dance, and that the dance was indecent, was one befitting a slave, and was performed by intoxicated persons. The Suidas *Lexicon (s.v.)* corroborates the first two of these points. The Townley Scholiast on *Iliad* 22.391 calls the dance "soft," and associates it with the *baukismos* and with the *schedismos*—the latter a lascivious dance or *schēma* the exact nature of which we do not know, but which may have been one of the figures of the *kordax.* The compiler of the *Etymologicum Magnum* (589.57, *s.v.* "mo-thōnia") implies that a characteristic of the *mothōn* may have been a swashbuckling strut. The *Lexicon* of Hesychius practically equates the words *mothōnas* and *mothakes,* and identifies them as servants (i.e., Helots) reared by the Spartans as companions to their sons. In the *Etymologicum Magnum* (590.4, *s.v.* "mothōn") a *mothōn* is defined as a house-born slave among the Spartans. Modern linguistic scholars[44] uphold the association of *mothōn* and *mothakes.* Athenaeus (6.271 E-F) tells us that the *mothakes* were slaves, but that they were treated as "foster brothers" of the Spartans, that they shared Spartan training, and that they were sometimes set free when they grew up. They were often called "master

---

[44] Cf. Boisacq (above, note 42), *s.v.* "mothōn."

seamen," he says—*despoinonautai*. Plutarch[45] tells how the Laconi-
ans annually forced the Helots to become intoxicated, to sing lewd
songs, and to dance low dances, as a horrible example to the young
Spartans.

One of the passages in which the *mothōn* is mentioned makes
use of a significant verb. "Apepydarisa *mothōna,*" says the Sau-
sage-Seller in the *Knights* of Aristophanes (697), deriding the
Paphlagonian and his threats. This is usually translated "I have
danced the *mothōn*"; but apparently *apopydarizō* means more
than just "dance." The scholiast on the passage implies that the
word denotes a dance in which the buttocks were struck with
the soles of the feet. Although the usage in this line of the *Knights*
is figurative, the *schēma* is a real one. Similar to it seems to have
been *rhathapygizein;* the *Lexicon* of Hesychius[46] defines this as
"to strike the buttocks with the feet bent back." Antyllus[47] says
that the kicking of the buttocks is done sometimes with both feet
together, sometimes with the feet alternating. He associates the
kicking *schēma* with the figures called *aphallesthai* and *exalles-
thai,* in the former of which the knees and body are bent far over,
and the dancer remains in one place, while in the latter the dancer
moves about. We are told by Pollux (4.102) that in Sparta the
buttock-kicking dance was called *bibasis;* that it was performed in
competition, by women or by children; and that the dancers who
executed the most kicks without stopping received prizes. The
Spartan Lampito boasts of her prowess in this type of dance in
Aristophanes' *Lysistrata* 82,[48] and some writers also see in lines
1310 and 1317 of the same play, where mention is made of frequent spirited leaps by Spartan maiden dancers, a suggestion of
the *bibasis*. Similar to the *bibasis* seems to have been the *schēma*
called *aposkelisai.*[49]

The scholiasts on Aristophanes' *Knights* 796 indicate that the
buttock-striking figure involves striking not only with the flat
of the foot, but with flat hand as well, with a great deal of accompanying noise, for comic effect. This recalls the *schēma* "flat

[45] *Lycurgus* 38.57.
[46] Hesychius *s.v.;* cf. also *s.v.* "halesthai pros pygēn."
[47] Ap. Oribasius 6.31.1.
[48] Cf. schol. ad loc.
[49] Hesychius *s.v.* "aposkelisai."

hand down," *cheir kataprēnēs*, which, as we have seen, is attested for the dance of tragedy. If the statements of the scholiasts are correct, it would seem that *cheir kataprēnēs* is used also in the dance of comedy. The statements would probably imply, in addition, the use in the *kordax* of *hekateris, hekaterides, hekaterein*, a figure which is mentioned by Athenaeus (14.630 A) in the same sentence with *cheir kataprēnēs, cheir simē, xylou paralēpsis*, and *kalathiskos*. The figure is explained in the *Lexicon* of Hesychius (*s.v.* "hekaterein") as "to leap towards the buttocks with one foot after the other"; and it is said by Pollux (4.102) to have been violent, and noteworthy for skillful movements of the hands. The underlying significance of the word *hekaterides* would seem to be a regular *alternation*, whether of hands or of feet.

In this connection an entry in the Hesychius *Lexicon* is interesting. It is *energeis*. Since the word is found nowhere else in Greek literature, various emendations have been suggested[50]—*energeia, energēsis, energis*—but none of these has been generally accepted. The word is defined as "the act of putting the hands down upon the buttocks." This gesture is common in painted representations upon the Corinthian vases often cited as related to the *kordax*.

In addition to buttock-kicking figures, other kicking figures certainly abounded in the dance of Old Comedy. Pollux mentions (4.102) *eklaktismata* as *orchēmata* (dance forms) of women, and says that in them "it was necessary to kick higher than the shoulder." The Hesychius *Lexicon* defines the *eklaktismos* (*s.v.*) as a violent (*syntonon*) *schēma* of the choral dance. That high kicking formed part of the dance of comedy is attested by Aristophanes' *Peace* 332. Also, male dancers use high kicks (*eklaktizein, skelos rhiptein*) in the concluding passage of the *Wasps* (1525)—"up to heaven" in lines 1492 and 1530.[51] In the same general category are the "turning" of the joints in their sockets, in *Wasps* 1495, and the swinging of the foot in a circle, in *Wasps* 1524. Even if, as seems likely, this concluding passage of the *Wasps* is a burlesque of the "new" dances sometimes introduced into the tragedy of Aristophanes' day, *schēmata* used in it merit attention as actually

---

[50] Cf. Latte (above, note 37), p. 20.
[51] See schol. ad loc. For a different interpretation of *skelos rhiptein*, here interpreted as a high kick, see Roos (above, note 1), pp. 176-178.

appearing in a comedy, and as possibly being themselves *schēmata* of the *kordax*.

We have discussed the likelihood that in the dance of comedy there was a figure in which the dancer slapped the buttocks with his hands. We have seen also that a slapping figure, of one sort or another, seems to have been used in the dance of tragedy. In this connection must be considered a dance *schēma* called *airein maschalēn*, "to lift the armpit."[52] We are told that it was used in rustic dancing and in "fun at a feast." Innumerable Greek vases, both red- and black-figured, show a great many representations of reveling dancers who "lift the armpit," bend the elbow at an acute angle, and hold the flat hand close to the dancer's body as if slapping the chest, ribs, thighs, buttocks, or stomach. All of these dancers hop, leap, or kick violently and spiritedly, and frequently the opened mouth of a dancer suggests singing or shouting. In the *exodos* of Aristophanes' *Wasps*, the chorus says (1529) to one of the "specialty dancers": "Gastrison seauton." This would seem to mean literally "Stomach yourself"—a command which some editors and translators have misinterpreted fantastically as "Kick yourself in the stomach" or "Hit your stomach with your heel!"[53] The Venetian Scholiast on the passage explains the order clearly as "Strike yourself on the stomach—a thing which [dancers] do while leaping."[54] An early red-figured psycter in the Louvre[55] shows the *schēma* very well.

Slapping figures and dances are found today, among many peoples. The Schuhplättler of Bavaria is one distinctive example—a lively, rollicking dance of men, in which the feet and legs are slapped in rhythm, with complicated and fascinating movements of the arms. Other slapping dances are to be seen in New Zealand, Samoa, and elsewhere around the Pacific. The underlying and original significance of such dances would seem to be a ritual

[52] Hesychius *s.v.*; Lillian B. Lawler, "*Airein Maschalēn* and Associated Orchestic *Schēmata*," *Transactions of the American Philological Association*, LXXX (1949), 230-237.
[53] *Aristophanes with the English Translation of Benjamin Bickley Rogers* (London and Cambridge, Mass., 1938), I, 549.
[54] Cf. Pollux 2.175; cf. also Aristophanes *Knights* 273, 454-455; *Clouds* 549; *Frogs* 1094-1096.
[55] Maurice Emmanuel, *Essai sur l'Orchestique Grecque* (Paris, 1895), Plate I, a and b, as frontispiece.

beating, to induce fertility, to drive out evil or sin, or merely to work off excess energy.[56] Thus they would seem to have an eminently appropriate place in Greek comedy and in the fertility dances which preceded it.

Rituals in which the performer did not beat himself, but was beaten by others, were likewise of great antiquity.[57] Here, too, the purpose was to stimulate the magic powers of life, to drive out evil, and to induce fertility. The dancer is like a carpet, we are told, which is beaten not to punish the carpet, but to get the dirt out of it. As time went on, the writhing of a dancer or an actor pretending to be or actually being flogged became conventionalized. In ancient Sparta, a ceremonial flogging is authenticated in connection with the cult of Artemis Orthia—evidently as a fertility charm.[58] In this cult and in others it often took the form of a food-stealing rite, in which young men tried to snatch from an altar, and eat, cheese, meat, wine, or cakes sacred to a divinity, and were ceremonially beaten with clubs or whips by attendants at the shrine. Theft, in and of itself, has some ritual importance. Rose[59] regards it as "part of a beneficent charm." Also, ritual stealing and beating is usually regarded as powerful magic, and is closely associated with purificatory rites among many peoples. It soon transforms itself, by a natural transition, into entertainment for the onlookers.

It is possible that food-stealing *schēmata* and dances may have

---

[56] Lillian B. Lawler, "Beating Motifs in the Greek Dance," *Classical Outlook*, XXI (1944), 59-61; Curt Sachs, *World History of the Dance* (New York, 1937), pp. 28, 38-39. Cf. the slapping of a torch racer during the festival of the Panathenaea by the spectators at the Cerameicus, "with flat hand," Aristophanes *Frogs* 1089-1098. In the motion picture "Pagan Love Song," released by Metro-Goldwyn-Mayer in 1950, and supposedly laid in Tahiti (and apparently filmed there), various native dances were shown. One was a solo dance performed by a man, with an accompaniment of drums. It was a spirited slap-dance. In it the dancer struck his body, all over, with many small slaps, throughout the dance. The slaps formed a clicking rhythm, somewhat reminiscent of the sound of tap dancing. Many of the postures assumed during the dance were very like those shown in the Louvre psycter referred to in note 55.

[57] Lillian B. Lawler, "The Dance of the Ancient Mariners," *Transactions of the American Philological Association*, LXXV (1944), 20-33.

[58] Plutarch *Lycurgus* 18.1; cf. 17.3; Xenophon *Lac.* 2.9; Alciphron *Epist.* 3.18.3.

[59] H. J. Rose, "Greek Rites of Stealing," *Harvard Theological Review*, XXXIV (1941), 1-5.

been used in comedy. The manuscripts of Athenaeus include (14.629 F) among "funny" dances, along with the *igdis, maktrismos, apokinos,* etc., something called the *chreōn apokopē,* which Cobet and others emended to *kreōn apoklopē,* "meat-stealing." Pollux (4.105) speaks of a *mimēlikēn* (generally emended to *mimētikēn*), in which the dancers imitated persons "caught in the act of stealing left-over meats" *(kreōn).* The *Lexicon* of Hesychius speaks of a "theft" dance, *klōpeia (s.v.),* which may refer to the same thing. The food-stealing (or wine-stealing) theme was a favorite one among the Spartan comic actors known as the *deikēlistai,*[60] and apparently also in the uproarious *"phlyakes* plays" of Southern Italy and Sicily. Representations of the food-stealing dance or *schēma* are seen by some scholars on a seventh-century Corinthian aryballos in the British Museum (A 1447); on a fragmentary sixth-century Boeotian kantharos in Leipzig; on a sixth-century Corinthian krater in the Louvre (E 632); on a vase in Leningrad; and on numerous other vases.[61] If, as seems likely, the four "birds" who enter separately in Aristophanes' *Birds* 266-293 are specialty dancers, there is a hint of a "gobbling dance" for one of them.[62] The theft of food or drink, often with accompanying or threatened violence, is mentioned very often in extant Old Comedy—e.g., in *Knights* 54-57, 101-102, 417-426, 744-745, 778, 822; *Frogs* 549-578; *Wasps* 60, where the taking away of food from Heracles is listed among stock themes of comedy; *Wasps* 448-452, 894-914; *Plutus* 680-681; and perhaps Epicharmus, fragment 239 (Kaibel), etc.

Beating, apart from food-stealing, also plays an important role in the production of Old Comedy.[63] Pollux (4.100) speaks of a "komastic" dance characterized by "fighting and blows." Aris-

---

60 Cf. Athenaeus 14.621 D-622 E; Pickard-Cambridge, *Dithyramb* (1st ed.; above, note 2), pp. 229-230, 253-259, 263-264; 268-277; Schnabel (above, note 1), pp. 49-54.

61 Erwin Bielefeld, *Komödienszene auf einem Griechischen Vasenbild* (Leipzig, 1944), with Abb. 1, 2, 3; Marcelle A. Hincks, "Le kordax dans le culte de Dionysos," *Revue Archéologique,* IV, Série 17 (1911), 1-5; Margarete Bieber, *The History of the Greek and Roman Theater* (2nd ed.; Princeton, 1961), Fig. 511, p. 140.

62 Lillian B. Lawler, "Four Dancers in the *Birds* of Aristophanes," *Transactions of the American Philological Association,* LXXIII (1942), 58-63; cf. Athenaeus 1.21 B.

63 Cf. Lawler, "Beating Motifs" (above, note 56), 59-61.

tophanes, in the *parabasis* of the *Clouds,* disclaiming the use of various stock situations of comedy, says (541-542) that in that particular play no old man "strikes his questioner with a stick"; and in *Peace* 741-748 he says that he has driven beatings from the comic theatre. Nevertheless, in every one of Aristophanes' extant plays a character or member of the chorus either beats or strikes another, or threatens to do so. One recalls, in particular, the famous beating scene in *Frogs* 605-673. In the *agōn* and elsewhere in a comedy, the chorus sometimes separates into two hostile bodies, and often exchanges threats or stages a mimetic combat which looks like a real fight—as in *Acharnians* 557-571; *Lysistrata* 352-387; 456-462; 658-705; 821-824. Also, the chorus as a whole often gets into a real or threatened fight with one or more actors—as in *Birds* 343-406; *Acharnians* 280-325; *Knights* 247-254; 453-456; *Wasps* 403-487. In the *Wasps* there is spirited fighting; cf. especially line 458—"Strike him with your stick!" In a choral passage of the *Birds* (1325-1328), the *choreutae* suggest that Peisthetaerus stir up his servant, "beating him like this"; quite evidently while singing they enact a beating, using their wings instead of weapons. Elsewhere the play abounds in beatings or threats of beatings; cf. 985, 1018, 1029-1031, 1043-1045, 1335-1336, 1402-1404, 1462-1466. It seems obvious that the *xylou paralēpsis,* attested for tragedy, and interpreted in our previous chapter as a gesture of "taking a club or staff" for mimetic enactment of beating or threatened violence, could have had a definite place also in comedy. It would be used in such passages as those mentioned, and also by persons recounting a story of a fight.

Leaping of all kinds seems to have been a commonplace in the dance of comedy. So were spirited turns—especially the *strobilos,* "whirlwind,"[64] and *bembikizein,* "spin like a top."[65] Also, the dance called the *phallikon,* with song of the same name,[66] may have appeared not only in the primitive ritual to Dionysus, not only in the capering of the performers in the various Dorian farces,[67] but also now and then in the dance of comedy in the classical period. Aristophanes in the *Clouds* (538-539) particularly includes the

---

[64] Athenaeus 14.630 A; Pollux 4.100; Aristophanes *Peace* 864.
[65] Aristophanes *Wasps* 1517; cf. 1530.
[66] Hesychius *s.v.* "phallikon"; Pollux 4.100.
[67] Cf. Athenaeus 14.621 F, 622 B-D.

phallic procession in his list of stock features of comedy which he will avoid; however, he does use it in his burlesque of the Rural Dionysia, in *Acharnians* 241-279.

We have observed in passing that in addition to the figures which are attested for the dance of Old Comedy, and those which very probably had a part in that dance, some of the figures ascribed by the lexicographers to the tragic dance seem to have been used in comedy as well. In fact, many scholars regard Pollux's use of the adjective *tragikos* as including comedy and the satyr play also, and as being equivalent to "dramatic."[68] We have already commented on the probable use in comedy of the "sword-thrust," *xiphismos;* of "flat hand down," *cheir kataprēnēs*, in buttock-striking and other slapping figures; and of "taking hold of a stick," *xylou paralēpsis*, in beating situations. The gesture called *cheir simē*, "hand bent up," has such a wide variety of uses in Greek art, and apparently in Greek life, that it would be difficult to exclude it from comedy. The violence of "the tongs," *thermaustris*, and "the split," *schisma* or *schistas helkein*, seems consistent with the nature of the *kordax*, but there is no specific mention of their use in any extant comedy. The *diplē*, attested as a *schēma* of the tragic dance by Pollux (4.105), is specifically called for in a choral passage of the *Thesmophoriazusae* (981-982); we shall consider it below.

"The basket," *kalathiskos*, called "tragic" by Pollux (4.105), and the apparently related *kalathismos* mentioned by Athenaeus (14.629 F), have already been discussed, in our previous chapter. A dance or figure performed by a person carrying a basket on his head might be appropriate also on occasion in comedy—as, e.g., briefly, in lines 641-642, 646-648, and 1193-1194 of the *Lysistrata* of Aristophanes; in the mock Dionysiac procession of *Acharnians* 241-279, and especially in 253-254, where the wife of Dicaeopolis bids her daughter carry the basket gracefully; and also perhaps in *Ecclesiazusae* 732 and *Birds* 1551. In this connection a representation on a bell krater in the Campanian style, now in the British Museum, is illuminating.[69] Here a male dancer identified

---

[68] Latte (above, note 37), p. 7.
[69] British Museum F 188. Cf. H. B. Walters, *Catalogue of the Greek and Etruscan Vases in the British Museum* (London, 1896), IV, 97; H. Heydemann, "Die phlyakendarstellungen auf bemahlten Vasen," *Jahrbuch des*

by Heydemann as a *phlyax* performer, by Cook as a *kalathiskos* dancer, bearing a large, shallow, basket-like object on his head, dances tipsily before a youthful Dionysus who stretches his hand toward the dancer, apparently offering him small objects which have usually been interpreted as fruits, but which may rather be cakes. (Cakes were sometimes offered to dancers in Greece.[70]) The bearded dancer is clad in a tight, sleeved "union suit" costume, and is wearing artificial breasts. He leans backward, with one foot raised to the front, and his center of gravity is obviously considerably disturbed. Although the vase painting does suggest a *phlyax* performance rather than a scene from a comedy, it indicates the possibility, at least, that on occasion the real "basket dances" or processions in religious ceremonies could be burlesqued.

The use in the *schēma* called *schistas helkein* of the verb *helkein*, meaning literally "draw, drag," is significant; for this verb and the related *helkyein* have figured extensively in an interpretation of the general nature of the *kordax* which had considerable vogue during the nineteenth century.[71] The impetus to the theory was furnished by two passages in Aristophanes—*Clouds* 540, in which the poet seems to say that this play of his has not "drawn the *kordax*," and *Peace* 328, in which the members of the chorus apparently beg Trygaeus to let them "draw"—*helkysai*—this one dance, and promise that they will then stop dancing and listen to him.[72] The use in these instances of a verb meaning "draw, drag," has interested commentators through many centuries. Scholiasts on *Clouds* 540 take the verb entirely figuratively, and define "draw the *kordax*" as "dance in an undignified manner." Farnabius, on the other hand, came to the conclusion that the *kordax* was a dance in which the dancer carried a rope, in memory of the rope by

---

deutschen archäologischen Instituts, I (1886), 290; Cook (above, note 5), III, Fig. 810 and p. 1000. Cook designates the krater as "in the style of Paestum." The catalogue identifies the vase as part of the Hamilton collecton, precise provenance unknown, but from Southern Italy or Magna Graecia.

[70] Athenaeus 14.647 C; 15.668 C, D; Plutarch *Quaest. conv.* 9.747 A; Demosthenes *De Cor.* 18.260; cf. Lillian B. Lawler, *"Orchēsis Iōnikē," Transactions of the American Philological Association,* LXXIV (1943), especially pp. 68-71.

[71] The theory is well summarized in Johannes Meursius' *"Orchestra,"* in the Gronovius *Thesaurus* (above, note 26) VIII, *s.v.* "kordax"; see also Schnabel (above, note 1), pp. 1-3.

[72] Cf. also *Clouds* 553.

[83]

which the wooden horse was pulled into Troy.[73] Donatus maintained that the "rope" was figurative, and was made up of the intertwined arms of the dancers, boys and girls side by side.[74] Farnabius cited in corroboration of his hypothesis Terence *Adelphi* 752-753, in which "Tu inter eas restim ductans saltabis"—"You will dance between them, drawing a rope"—is the remark made to a man who is proposing to install in the same house both his son's wife and a courtesan; and the man replies, "Et tu nobiscum una, si opus est"—"And you along with us, if there is need." Other passages cited by the followers of Farnabius were Petronius *Cena* 52, in which Trimalchio says of his wife, ". . . cordacem nemo melius ducit"—"no one draws the *cordax* better"; and Livy 27. 37. 12-15, an account of a Roman expiatory ritual during the Second Punic War, in which twenty-seven maidens holding a rope in their hands—"per manus reste data"—sang and danced—"sonum vocis pulsu pedum modulantes incesserunt"—and then moved in procession to the temple of Juno Regina.

Starting from the Farnabius theory,[75] Cook went on to cite a famous fresco from Mycenae in which ass-headed figures carry on their shoulders something which most observers interpret as a pole, but which he called a rope. Cook collected an interesting body of evidence of the association of asses, ropes, and water, and concluded that the *kordax* had originated in prehistoric times in a ritual rope-carrying dance of ass-masked votaries in honor of spirits of moisture and fertility; and that the ritual had subsequently passed into the cult of Dionysus.

The Greeks did have some dances in which rope-like objects were carried. Elsewhere[76] I have expressed my own belief that the famous winding *geranos* dance of Delos was of this nature; that, in it, dancers originally carried a representation of a very large snake; that in later times these representations became rope-like or cable-like objects; that ultimately the intermeshed arms of the dancers replaced these objects; and that this dance influ-

---

[73] Farnabius' note may be seen in *Publi Terentii Carthaginiensis Afri Comoediae* (Amsterdam, 1686), VI, on lines 752-753 of the *Adelphi*.

[74] See Meursius (above, note 71), *s.v.* "kordax."

[75] A. B. Cook, "Animal Worship in the Mycenaean Age—I, The Cult of the Ass," *Journal of Hellenic Studies*, XIV (1894), 81-102.

[76] Lillian B. Lawler, "The *Geranos* Dance," *Transactions of the American Philological Association*, LXXVII (1946), 112-130.

enced many other Greek dances. We have already noted the possibility that the dithyrambic dance may have been so influenced. The garland-carrying processional dance of the Hellotia[77] was of the same general type. It seems evident that the passage in Terence is a joking and metaphorical reference to one of these dances, probably the *geranos;* and that the dance in Livy is an old serpentine dance of the *geranos* type, dedicated to a mother goddess. But there seems to be no evidence whatsoever of the rope-carrying motif in the *kordax.* It is true that Aristophanes has Lysistrata, in the play of the same name, 1274-1276, arrange the Athenians and their wives, and probably the Spartans also, alternately in the dance line, in the "mixed" or *anamix* arrangement, as the Greeks called it, which is said to have been characteristic of the *geranos;* and that in their brief dance (1279-1294) they probably imitated the *geranos.* But, as we shall see later, this dance is clearly not the *kordax.*

The whole theory, of course, turns upon the significance of the words *helkein, helkyein,* "draw"; and I believe that the scholiasts are entirely correct in interpreting their usage in the passages cited as metaphorical, not literal. A substantive related to *helkein,* viz., *holkos,* is used metaphorically of the trailing length of a snake, in Nicander's *Theriaca* (162, 166, 226, 266, 296, 316). It is entirely natural for a verb meaning literally "drag, draw" to be used figuratively of a dance (cf. our own "Varsity Drag" of some years ago); this is true even if the basic step of the dance is not slow or "dragging." Such a usage is common in the case of the Latin words *ducere, ductare, pedem trahere.* I believe, then, that we have no ground for interpreting the *kordax* as a rope dance; and I believe we must translate *helkyein* in the Aristophanes passages simply as *"perform* the *kordax."*

As for Cook's theory that the *kordax* is an ass dance, a careful scrutiny of the nature and sources of the dance would seem to refute such a hypothesis. It is true that one writer of Old Comedy, Archippus, did produce a play called *Onos,* "The Ass." But it appears to have been of no more significance for the *kordax* than any one of several comedies with animal titles. We have no literary

---

[77] Athenaeus 15.678 A; *Et. Mag. s.v.* "Hellotia"; Schol. Pindar *Olymp.* 13.56; cf. Hesychius *s.vv.* "Hellotia," "Hellotis." Cf. Lillian B. Lawler, "A Necklace for Eileithyia," *Classical Weekly,* XLII (1948), 2-6.

evidence of an ass dance or *schēma*, within or without the orbit of the *kordax*.

Like other dances of the theatre, the *kordax* was performed to the music of the flute. We have a list of various types of flute music which accompanied dancing—a list compiled by Tryphon and preserved in the work of Athenaeus (14.618 C). If we may judge by the names of these musical types, several of them might well accompany the *kordax*. These are: the *kōmos*, and perhaps also the *tetrakōmos;* the *epiphallos;* possibly the "knocking at the door," *thyrokopikon* or *krousithyron;* and the *mothōn*. Immediately preceding the *mothōn* is a musical type known as the *knismos*, "the itch." Pollux (4.100), Eustathius (1236.57), and the *Lexicon* of Hesychius *(s.v.)* also name it, but give no further information about it. It is tempting to conjecture that it, too, may have had a place in the *kordax*.

Musical instruments other than the flute seem to have been used occasionally in comedy. In a much disputed passage in the *Acharnians* (862-863), a Boeotian enters accompanied by some "musicians from Thebes" who play upon instruments which seem to be bagpipes made of dog-skin and dogs' bones. The musicians play an interlude, and are then dismissed. Such instruments are exceptional in the theatre of the classical period, and are obviously introduced for their humorous effect. Again, in *Lysistrata* 1242 and 1245, "pipes" of some kind—*physatēria, physallides*—are mentioned, and probably actually used, as accompaniment to a Spartan dance.

Certainly not all dancing in comedy came under the category of the *kordax*. It appears that comedy, like tragedy, was enriched with colorful dances and *schēmata* of many sorts, appropriate to the plots of the several plays. In the case of comedy, however, we can be sure that many of these are not a part of the *kordax*, the distinctive dance of the genre, for of it we have rather precise definitions, as we do not have for the *emmeleia* of tragedy.

Among these "enriching" dances and figures are many imitating or suggesting animals and birds. In view of the antiquity of animal mummery in the Greek world, this is not surprising. The titles of many comedies in themselves imply, although they do not attest with certainty, choruses of animal mummers. We might instance here the *Birds* of Aristophanes, of Crates, and of Magnes;

[86]

the *Nightingales* of Cantharus; the *Storks* and *Wasps* of Aristophanes; the *Bees* of Diocles; the *Gall-Flies* of Magnes; the *Fishes* of Archippus; the *Frogs* of Callias and of Magnes; the *Goats* of Eupolis; the *Swine* of Cephisodorus; the *Griffins* of Plato; and the *Beasts* of Crates. There may have been other plays based on animal motifs, of which even the titles are now lost to us. The general appearance of the choruses in such plays, elaborately masked and garbed, may be conjectured from vase paintings;[78] and the way in which animal dances fitted into the plays can be well understood from the texts of the *Birds* and the *Wasps* of Aristophanes. To be sure, we cannot go too far in speculation on the dances in the lost plays; for the extant *Frogs* of Aristophanes, in which some scholars believe that the frogs did not even appear to the audience, but merely sang off-scene, warns us to be cautious!

Most extensively used of the animal *schēmata* in existing specimens of Old Comedy seem to be those concerned with birds and flying. We have already seen that such *schēmata* apparently had a place in tragedy also. Quite naturally the *Birds* of Aristophanes abounds in flying motifs and gestures. In it, many characters express a desire to "fly through the air"; and gestures of flying could appropriately accompany their words, and also the "high-flown" lines of Cinesias (1372-1409). It is possible that the four birds who enter separately (266-293) just before the entrance of the chorus—the flame-colored bird, the cock, the grandson of the Hoopoe, and the "gobbler"—may be four "specialty dancers."[79] Furthermore, the elaborateness of the conclusion of the play (1720-1765), which combines features of a nuptial procession with those of a *kallinikos* or victory procession, is further heightened by something which suggests the *volador*, or "flying dance" of Mexico, in which the dancers are suspended from poles by cords, and "dance" in the air. Peisthetaerus, now winged, bids his bride stretch out her hand, take hold of his wings, and dance with him, as he lifts her into the air (1759-1762). Here the simple lifting device of the Attic theatre known as the "crane" may have been employed effectively.

Bird *schēmata* appear or are referred to in other plays as well.

---

[78] See Roy C. Flickinger, *The Greek Theater and Its Drama* (4th ed.; Chicago, 1936), *Figs.* 12-16, pp. 32-40.

[79] Cf. Lawler, "Four Dancers" (above, note 62).

[87]

A cuckoo dance is mentioned in *Knights* 697; and although the reference is probably only a passing one, in the form of a metaphor, such a dance seems to have existed.[80]

A figure associated with a cock—although its connection with the bird seems slightly nebulous—and called variously *ptēssein* or *oklasma*, is used in the *Wasps* (1490) and perhaps in the *Knights* (495-497). This figure (and also the dance in which it appears) is sometimes known as "the Persian," just as the cock is often called "the Persian bird." Pollux (4.100) tells us that the *oklasma* is "komastic," vigorous, and *hygron*—the latter word implying suppleness. Apparently the dancing-girl in Aristophanes' *Thesmophoriazusae* (1175 and schol. ad loc.) makes use of "the Persian." Xenophon[81] records an occasion when a Mysian carrying a shield in each hand performs the "Persian": . . . "striking the shields together; and he *ōklaze* (crouched) and then arose again; and he did all these things in rhythm, to the flute."[82] The figure must have been in general similar to the modern Russian "squat, fling" knee dance.

Among other animal dances found incidentally in comedy are those of the chorus in the peculiar pantomime-like interlude in the *Plutus* (290-315) in which Cario dances the parts of Polyphemus and Circe, and members of the chorus caper about as sheep, goats, and swine.

Sometimes the poet inserts into the framework of the comedy a dance or a rhythmic procession intended to convey the impression of some important religious ritual. Of this type is the burlesque of the Rural Dionysia in the *Acharnians* (241-279), in which Dicaeopolis, his daughter, and his slave Xanthias carry sacred objects and invoke Dionysus. In the *Thesmophoriazusae* (947-1000) Aristophanes purports to set forth, in the evolutions of the chorus, steps and movements of the secret dances of the Thesmophoria. Needless to say, he would neither have been familiar with, nor have dared to reproduce, actual dances of the women at that secret festival; he would probably have recalled vividly the charge of impiety which was brought against Aeschylus for

---

[80] Lillian B. Lawler, "Periekokkasa—*Knights* 697," *American Journal of Philology*, LXXII (1951), 300-307.

[81] Xenophon *Anab.* 6.1.10.

[82] Roos (above, note 1), pp. 66-68, has a good discussion of "the Persian."

having divulged in one of his plays the sacred mysteries of Demeter.[83] What he really does in the *Thesmophoriazusae* is to portray a rapid circle dance with the dancers holding hands (958-
980); then a *diplē,* or "double" dance (981-984), probably a figure
in which the chorus divides into two semi-choruses, dancing in
opposition to one another; and finally a restrained and classic
version of a Bacchic dance (987-1000), evidently as a formal
tribute to Dionysus as god of the theatre.[84] In the *Frogs* (316-459)
the playwright again suggests the dances of a ritual—this time the
Eleusinian Mysteries. Here the members of the chorus march in
stately procession, bearing torches and calling upon Iacchus and
other divinities to join them or to be favorable to them; they then
proceed to an imaginary flowery meadow where they dance in
a circle (441). In the passage there are hints of the *gephyrismos,*
the ritual invective (416-430), and the *pannychides,* the all-night
songs and dances (371), which featured the real Mysteries. However, since the presence of these motifs in the Eleusinian ritual
was a matter of common knowledge, Aristophanes could safely
refer to them in his play.

Ritual processions and dances of other types are also introduced into comedies. The *paean,* or solemn processional hymn to
a divinity, is sometimes suggested—as in Aristophanes' *Peace* 555-
559 and 582-602, and *Wasps* 863-874. Various invoking songs and
dances appear in many plays—e.g., in Aristophanes' *Thesmophoriazusae* 1136-1159, *Lysistrata* 1262-1272, and *Peace* 974-992.

There is considerable evidence[85] that a "seeking, searching"
motif is a common one in the dramatic performances and dances—
especially in those of the satyr play, but in those of comedy as well.
Also, it is known[86] that a characteristic feature of the secret ritual
of the *Thesmophoria* was a ceremonial "chasing away" of somebody—the *diōgma* or *apodiōgma.* Presumably in this chase the
women sought out any men who might be in the vicinity of their

---

[83] Aelian *Var. Hist.* 5.19; Aristotle *Nic. Eth.* 3.1.17.1111 A.
[84] Cf. Lawler, *"Diplē"* (above, note 27).
[85] Lillian B. Lawler, "The Dance of the Owl," *Transactions of the American
Philological Association,* LXX (1939), 500-502; "Blinding Radiance and
the Greek Dance," *Classical Journal,* XXXVII (1941), 94-96.
[86] Hesychius *s.v.* "diōgma." Pickard-Cambridge, *Dithyramb* (1st ed.;
above, note 2), p. 140, says that "ritual pursuit and bloodshed (real or
feigned) is a common form of agrarian magic."

dancing place, and drove them away. In the *Thesmophoriazusae* (685-687) the members of the chorus gird up their garments and engage in a systematic search for the intruder against whom they have been warned. During the search they very probably use the peering gesture, the *skopos* (667), in which the eyes are shaded with the hand. Later in the play (953-959) the *choreutae*, performing a circle dance, "look on all sides," sweeping the whole horizon in the course of the dance.[87] The peering gesture, the *skopos*, could be used in many other plays—e.g., in the *Plutus* (99), the *Acharnians* (204-207), the *Knights* (170-175, 312, and 419-420), the *Ecclesiazusae* (480-481), the *Clouds* (323-327 and 342-343). Here we recall that gestures used to interpret speech in a play are thought of as a kind of dancing. The pursuit motif is found similarly in other plays—e.g., in the *Acharnians* (204-236), the *Clouds* (1508), and the *Knights* (247-252).

We have noted that there is some emphasis in tragedy on gestures suggestive of oars and rowing. Similar gestures might be used in comedy, especially in the *Frogs* (202-269), and perhaps also in the *Knights* (541-546, 554-555, 830) and in the *Wasps* (1091-1101).

Other gestures have a place in comedy. In *Thesmophoriazusae* 163, for example, Agathon, after saying that a poet should never be harsh, cites various writers of lyric poetry of whom he approves, and says that they used Ionian dances and motifs, and "moved thus"—evidently illustrating the soft, voluptuous gestures briefly as he speaks.[88]

In our consideration of the dances of tragedy, we have noted evidence that there appeared occasionally in it a brief *hyporchēma* —a lively, joyous choral dance, with strong mimetic gestures, usually introduced rather suddenly. Apparently of this same type is the dance in the *Peace* 321-336 and elsewhere; possibly one was also introduced in the *Plutus*, just after 760-763.

Athenaeus speaks several times[89] of a playwright named Callias, who is known to have lived in the last third of the fifth century B.C., and who wrote a *grammatikē tragoedia*—a play about the letters of the alphabet—parts of which Athenaeus quotes. The so-

---

[87] Lawler, *"Diplē,"* (above, note 27), 60-61.
[88] Cf. Horace *Carm.* 3.6.21-24.
[89] Athenaeus 7.276 A; 10.448 B; 453 C-F.

called "spectacle of the letters"[90] had a "prologue" (in verse, of course) composed of the names of the letters of the Ionic alphabet. It also had a chorus of women who sang, to musical accompaniment, strophes in lyric meter which were simply exercises in syllabification—e.g., "Beta alpha, ba," etc. After this choral passage there was a speech by the vowels. Athenaeus says further (10.453 E-454 A) that Callias was the first to describe the shapes of the letters in iambic verse. He gives as an example a passage, very much in the manner of Attic comedy, in which the letters psi and omega are described; whether this passage is from the *grammatikē tragoedia* or not we do not know.

The Athenaeus passages have given rise to endless discussion. Some scholars regard the play as an actual comedy, with the twenty-four letters of the Ionic alphabet forming the comic chorus of twenty-four. Others think the whole thing was a *tour de force,* perhaps never to be produced at all. The Ionic alphabet was not formally adopted at Athens until 403 b.c., but it certainly was in common use at Athens, and there was a fair amount of interest in it, for some time before the formal adoption.

If the play of Callias was ever produced, we may take it as certain that some form of "alphabet dance" appeared in it; and, as a matter of fact, Athenaeus (14.629 F) actually mentions a dance called *stoicheia,* "the letters," in his list of "amusing" dances.

Following the discussion of Callias' play in Athenaeus there is mention of a related phenomenon—the description by an illiterate character in a play of the shapes of letters which he has seen and remembered, but cannot read. Athenaeus cites three instances of this device in tragedy, all of them connected with the letters that spell the name Theseus. Here the character probably used gestures to make "pictures in the air" resembling the shapes of the letters. It is not known whether such "pictures in the air" were used in the play of Callias or whether, perhaps, the members of the chorus made letter-like formations, as rooters do in our

---

[90] Cf. Peter D. Arnott, "The *Alphabet Tragedy* of Callias," *Classical Philology,* LV (1960), 178-180; Lillian B. Lawler, "The Dance of the Alphabet," *Classical Outlook,* XVIII (1941), 69-71. Cf. Cornelia Meigs, *Invincible Louisa* (Boston, 1945), p. 38, for a modern attempt at representing the letters of the alphabet by means of contortions of the body.

football stadia today, or whether each member of the chorus impersonated a separate letter. We can only conjecture that there may have been in the play some form of "alphabet mummery."

Victory dances of one sort or another appear frequently in Old Comedy. For the most part they take the form of the *kallinikos,* a dance which appears also in tragedy. Essentially a dance of the *kōmos* type, the *kallinikos* lends itself well to performance in the drama. It consists, in the main, of walking or running, with gestures appropriate to the song being sung.[91]

The *Acharnians* concludes (1227-1234) with a victory song which is a direct parody and echo of the famous victory song by Archilochus (frag. 119 Bergk), in which the twanging of the strings of a lyre was imitated by the word *tēnella.* Sung by Dicaeopolis and the chorus in alternation, it is avowedly a song of rejoicing over the former's victory in a drinking contest; but actually it is staged as "wishful thinking," as it were, in the hope of victory in the dramatic competition. The dance accompanying the victory song is here clearly a processional one. Somewhat similarly, the *Birds* ends (1763-1765) with a song of victory in which appear the words *tēnella kallinikos.* The accompanying dance is again processional; in this case it is both a nuptial and a victory dance, as the chorus follows the victorious Peisthetaerus and his newly-won bride. The *Peace* also ends with a combined nuptial and victory dance (1316-1357), but with no specific use of the word *kallinikos.* Trygaeus (1355-1357), bidding the chorus follow him, promises cakes to one and all.

The *Knights* ends with no victory dance, but rather with an invitation to the chorus to follow Demos to a feast. However, in an earlier part of the play (581-594) the chorus sings a prayer to Athena for victory in the dramatic competition.

The *Ecclesiazusae* ends (1168-1183) with a joyous dance of the women who have won their victory in the Assembly and put their "new order" into effect. Instead of the word *kallinikos,* they use in their dance-song the phrase "hōs epi nikē"—"thus for victory"—expressing thereby the poet's hope for a victory in the dramatic competition (1182). (The phrase, as we have seen, is used also

---

[91] Cf. Lillian B. Lawler, *"Orchēsis Kallinikos," Transactions of the American Philological Association,* LIX (1948), 254-267. See also the discussion of this dance in our preceding chapter.

in connection with the dance of tragedy.) The celebration is therefore twofold—a jollification over the victory already attained by the women in the play, and a preview of the festivities which will attend the hoped-for dramatic victory of the author. As in the case of many other plays, the *choreutae* dance out to a feast.

Almost the same words are found in a dance-song in the *Lysistrata* (1279-1294), although not precisely at the end of the play. The chorus of Athenian men and women sing and dance "hōs epi nikē," "thus for victory" (1293). Again there are two victories involved—the tactical victory won by Lysistrata in the play, and the desired victory of Aristophanes in the comic contest. For the dance, Lysistrata carefully arranges the dancers *anamix*—i.e., a man and a woman, alternating side by side (1271-1278), and apparently holding hands. This mingling of men and women in the dance, the so-called *geranos* formation,[92] was not common in the classical period. The arrangement gives us a choreography very different from that of the processional victory dances we have been observing in other plays. We shall consider it further below.

Akin to, but not identical with, the victory dance at the end of the play is the joyous "escorting" dance. The *Plutus* ends (1194-1209) with a festive procession bearing torches and accompanying Wealth to his former home on the Acropolis. The *Frogs* is concluded (1528-1533) with a torch-bearing procession in which the members of the chorus, singing lines inspired by his own poetry, accompany Aeschylus upon the start of his journey to the upper world. Here we may recall that a similar escorting dance was used by Aeschylus himself in the *exodos* of his tragedy *Eumenides* (1003-1047). There Athena leads a torch-bearing procession of priests, attendants, and members of the Court of the Areopagus which, singing as it goes, accompanies the Eumenides to their new home. Basically the escorting dance is a form of the *kōmos*.

As we have noted, there has been much controversy over the *exodos* of the *Wasps*.[93] We have expressed agreement with the

---

[92] Cf. Lillian B. Lawler, "The *Geranos* Dance," *Transactions of the American Philological Association*, LXXVII (1946), 112-130.

[93] Roos (above, note 1) holds that the dances there portrayed and mentioned were originally dances of courtesans and drunken youths.

[93]

scholars who regard the dance there as an uproarious burlesque of some of the "new" dances introduced into tragedy by playwrights of Aristophanes' own day. Also, we have seen, in the particular *schēmata* used, various lewd figures which are common to the *kordax*, the *sikinnis*, rituals to fertility divinities, and dances of courtesans. Lucian (*Salt.* 26) implies that in comedy the *kordax* was indeed sometimes supplemented with the *sikinnis*, although the latter is properly the dance of the satyr play.

As the members of the chorus leave the *orchēstra* in the *Wasps* (1535-1537), they invite the solo dancers who have just been performing to lead them out dancing, a thing which, they say, no one has done before in comedy. This passage has aroused much speculation, since in many of the extant plays of Aristophanes an actor does seem to do just that. Some scholars have conjectured that in the *exodos* the chorus was customarily regarded as marching rather than dancing. However, to a Greek a rhythmical march was certainly a form of dancing. The statement of the chorus may indeed be ironical—somewhat after the manner of Gilbert and Sullivan's Captain of the *Pinafore*, perhaps, who is "*never, never* sick at sea"—since a spirited dance with an actor in the lead would seem to have formed a stereotyped finale in Old Comedy.

There has been disagreement over aspects of the dance in the *exodos* of one or two other comedies of Aristophanes. In the *Ecclesiazusae* (1165-1166), just before the chorus goes out, ostensibly to dinner, somebody—editors assign the words variously to a semi-chorus, to the full chorus or its *coryphaeus*, or to a maid-servant—says, giving directions for the dance steps to follow, "And you, too, move your feet in the Cretan manner." Some of the interpretations of the words have been (1) that the command is a jest, poking fun at the greediness of the Cretans; (2) that the reference is to meter—"Cretan rhythms"; (3) that a Cretan *hyporchēma* is indicated at this point. Actually, literary and archaeological evidence seems to indicate that the expression denotes a proud and vigorous "high-stepping" on the part of the dancers. In line 1167 apparently the "little girls," *meirakes*, who accompany the chorus, are bidden to mark the rhythm "with the whole leg"; and in line 1179 the members of the chorus cry, to one another, "Be lifted up high"—*airesth' anō*—as they leave the *orchēstra* at a lively pace. Such spirited dancing, with marked lifting of the

[94]

leg, and with the back straight and the head held high, seems to have been a feature of processional dances among the Minoan Cretans.[94]

The conclusion of the *Lysistrata* has furnished material for further discussion and disagreement. The scene is one of re-joicing; peace has been made, a great feast has been consumed, and both Athenians and Spartans are preparing to dance in cele-bration. One of the Spartans addresses a girl musician: "Take your pipes *(physatēria)*, my dear," he says, "so that I may dance the *dipodia*, and sing a fair song for the Athenians and for us, at the same time" (1242-1244). An Athenian expresses approval, and says that he enjoys watching the Spartan dance (1245-1246). The Spartan then obliges, with a dance and song in praise of the great deeds of both Athenians and Spartans in the Persian War, and in invocation of Artemis as virgin huntress (1247-1272). Editors and translators of the play show a variety of interpretations of the pas-sage. Clearly the *dipodia* referred to is not a violent, lewd, or gro-tesque dance. A fragment of Cratinus (*Plut.* 5 Meineke; 162 Kock) reads "for he will begin the *dipodia* beautifully." In both cases the emphasis is on beauty *(kalōn, kalōs);* and in the *Lysistrata* the dance accompanies a dignified song on a lofty theme. It seems to have been a graceful dance, suitable for a joyous occasion, yet restrained in style. Its name may show an original connection with the trochaic *dipodia* or dimeter, a common meter in Spartan choral songs.[95]

After the performance of the *dipodia*, Lysistrata, as we have seen, arranges the whole company in couples, a man and a woman side by side, and bids them dance in that formation (1273-1277). They comply, the Athenians first calling upon their gods and goddesses in Attic Greek (1279-1295). The Spartans follow, with a similar song in the Laconian dialect (1296-1322), praising Sparta and invoking her divinities. In most dances of this alignment, both ancient and modern (including the ancient *geranos* and the modern *tratta*), the performers hold hands, often with arms crossed or enmeshed, and dance in a long line. Dances of this sort can be seen to this day in all parts of Greece, and in Southern

---

[94] Cf. Lillian B. Lawler, *"Krētikōs* in the Greek Dance," *Transactions of the American Philological Association*, LXXXII (1952), 62-70.

[95] Cf. Lawler, *"Diplē,"* (above, note 27).

[95]

Italy as well, particularly at village festivals. In them the dancers move forward and backward, and at the same time toward the right, in a graceful, balancing pattern. Frequently the men disengage their hands and indulge in more vigorous movements than those of the women, leaping high and turning rapidly, then rejoin hands and move on as before.

Apart from dances and figures actually performed or suggested during the course of the plays, it is interesting that Old Comedy is for us a source of information on several dances which are mentioned in passing. One of these may be the cuckoo dance mentioned in *Knights* 697, of which we have already taken account. Another is the *arkteia*, the ritual bear dance performed in propitiation of the Brauronian Artemis, by little girls in yellow-brown "bear" costumes.[96] A third is the *askōliasmos*, a dance performed in competition, probably at the Rural Dionysia; in it the dancer hopped on one leg upon an inflated and greased wine-skin or bladder.[97] Still others are the ecstatic song and dance to the hand-drum or *tympanon*, performed by women in honor of the Phrygian god Sabazius, akin to Dionysus, and the songs and dances performed by women on the rooftops of their houses in lamentation for the dead divinity Adonis.[98]

Another dance mentioned by a character in the *Lysistrata* (408-413) is sometimes erroneously interpreted as a social dance, almost in the modern manner. A husband, speaking to a goldsmith, tells him that his wife, dancing the evening before, has lost the clasp of her necklace. There is no evidence here at all for a couple dance; the reference is probably to one of the many ritual dances which lasted all night[99]—particularly the nativity dances performed by women on the tenth day of a child's life.

Interestingly, Old Comedy also furnishes us with an example of the metaphorical use of the word "dance"—*orcheisthai*—to denote earnest activity. "I will never weary of dancing," say the chorus of women in the *Lysistrata* (541-542), "and my knees will not tire." They refer not to actual dancing, but to the determined carrying out of Lysistrata's plans.

---

96 *Lysistrata* 645; cf. Farnell (above, note 19), II, 436-442.
97 *Plutus* 1129; cf. Pollux 9.121.
98 *Lysistrata* 387-394.
99 Athenaeus 14.647 C; 15.668 C, D; cf. Lillian B. Lawler, "She Could Have Danced All Night," *Classical Outlook*, XXXIV (1957), 54-55.

Toward the close of the fifth century, many changes began to be evident in Athenian comedy.

Athens was in the throes of a long and wearying war with Sparta. Increasing costs had made it difficult to secure *chorēgi* for plays; accordingly, a system of *synchorēgia* was instituted, permitting two or more persons to share in the cost of costuming and training each comic chorus. The immediate result of this change was an increased enthusiasm for comedy; ultimately the number of such plays produced at a festival was raised from three to five.[100] Still later, in the fourth century, the state assumed a large share of the cost of the dramatic performances.

Also, various changes occurred within the plays themselves. Plots became less topical, less political. Attacks on real, living persons gave way to hits at imaginary persons, persons long dead, or "types." Ribald obscenity weakened to *double entendre* and risqué insinuations. With the fall of Athens to Sparta, the bold freedom of speech of the earlier writers became a thing of the past.

Meanwhile, the treatment of the chorus underwent a change. Even in the lifetime of Aristophanes, the *parabasis*, the direct address of the chorus to the audience, began to disappear; and three of his plays, the *Lysistrata*, the *Ecclesiazusae*, and the *Plutus*, contain no *parabasis*. Shorter and shorter choral odes replace the longer ones; the lyrics vanish, and the script bears only the word *chorou*—"of the chorus"—at points where we should expect to find choral odes. The last two extant plays of Aristophanes, the *Ecclesiazusae* and the *Plutus*, show this characteristic of their time, also. Some scholars think that the chorus merely danced to flute music during these interludes. Others think that any appropriate or popular songs might be here introduced. Still others think that the poet wrote lyrics for use at these points, but that they were regarded as of so little importance that they were omitted when the plays were prepared for "publication." In time the chorus becomes merely a small group of singers—usually a *kōmos* of revelers, connected loosely if at all with the plot of the play; they enter, sing and perform some sort of revel dance as an interlude between

---

100 Pickard-Cambridge, *Dramatic Festivals* (above, note 1), p. 88, thinks that the use of *synchorēgi* at the City Dionysia was confined to one year only, 406/405 B.C., and, p. 84, that in classical times there were five writers of comedy in competition at the City Dionysia except during part of the Peloponnesian War, when the number was temporarily reduced to three.

the episodes of the play, and then leave. We have noted the use of similar interludes, called *embolima*, in tragedy. Even the very nature of the music changed, and florid trills and novelties, produced on a variety of instruments, replaced the more severe and restrained measures of the flute which had been universal in the earlier performances.

We have now come to the period known as that of Middle Comedy—approximately the first half of the fourth century B.C. It is really a transitional age, between Old and New Comedy, and seems to have been one of little vitality or creative ability. We have the names of many of the writers of Middle Comedy—e.g., Alexis, Antiphanes, Anaxandrides, Eubulus, Heniochus—but not one of their plays has survived. From what other Greek writers say of them, we know that their plots were allegorical, mythological, even rhetorical, and lacked the zest of Old Comedy. We hear of choruses of fifteen members, of eleven members, or even fewer, in their plays. However, the illusion of Old Comedy was retained; and some scholars believe that during this period many of the plays of Aristophanes and his contemporaries were revised and produced in the style of the day.

New comedy develops after the middle of the fourth century, and soon routs Middle Comedy. New Comedy is, of course, a comedy of manners, with much emphasis on plot. The outstanding writer of plays in this genre is the Athenian Menander. We have rather considerable fragments of some of his plays; and very recently, in a private collection in Switzerland, a virtually complete copy of his *Dyskolos*, or "Bad-Tempered Man," came to light, in a papyrus manuscript dating from the first half of the third century of the Christian era.[101]

By the very nature of New Comedy there is little place in it for a chorus which was so outstanding a feature of Old Comedy. Also, the introduction of a stage into the theatre, and the transfer of the action from the *orchēstra* to the stage, had cut down on the evolutions of the chorus in all forms of the drama. It is true that

---

[101] *Papyrus Bodmer IV, Ménandre: Le Dyscolos,* Publié par Victor Martin (Geneva, 1958). The English translation by Gilbert Highet, under the title "The Curmudgeon," may be found in the magazine *Horizon,* I (1959), 78-88; another, by W. G. Arnott, under the title *Menander's Dyskolos, or The Man Who Didn't Like People,* was published by the University of London, 1960.

in one of Menander's plays, *The Hero,* a band of huntsmen forms a sort of vestigial chorus, but even in cases such as this the actual connection of the chorus with the play must have been very slight. As a result, dancing is of comparatively little importance in New Comedy. The chorus seems to be almost always a *kōmos*—a group of noisy revelers going to or coming from a feast. They sing and dance, usually between the "acts" of the play—for in New Comedy a division into five acts was soon adopted. Their songs do not appear in the plays or fragments which we have, and only the word *chorou* signals their entrance. In the *Dyskolos* four such choral interludes are indicated—after lines 232, 426, 619, and 783 of the papyrus. In the first of these instances, one of the characters, Daos, heralds the approach of the revelers in the following words (lines 230-232): ". . . For I see some devotees of Pan coming this way, just a bit drunk, and it seems to me that it isn't the right time to get into any trouble with them." The word *chorou* then appears. The three other entrances of the chorus are introduced by *chorou* without comment by any of the actors. There are five passages in extant parts of other plays by Menander in which *chorou* is used similarly. At the conclusion of the *Dyskolos* (954-969), the misanthrope is dragged, protesting, into revels, presumably including dancing, which may or may not be performed in sight of the audience, as the play ends.

Apparently on occasion a dance by one or more of the characters in the play may be introduced into New Comedy. In a fragment of the *Theophoroumenē* of Menander, in which two men are shown as suspicious of the divine frenzy of the "possessed maiden" for whom the play is named, one suggests to the other that if her ecstatic state is real, the music of a flute will cause her to dance after the manner of the Corybantes. They bid the flutist play, and then withdraw so as to observe the results, unseen. Unfortunately the fragment ends at that point, and we do not know whether the dance was actually performed or not. Also, a dancing-girl appears now and then among the characters in New Comedy, and we may conjecture that she performed at some point in the play.

In three of the plays of Plautus—*Bacchides, Poenulus,* and *Rudens*—all modeled closely upon Greek New Comedy, there are hints of choruses of a sort. In the first there is a suggestion of a *kōmos;* in the second there is a group of "advocates"; in the third there is a group of fishermen. However, they are not true choruses in the real sense of the word, but rather merely a group of actors. Scholars have noted also that Terence's play *Heautontimoroumenos* shows at line 172 a trace of a chorus of banqueters in the original from which the play was derived, and at line 745 a hint of a chorus of maid-servants.

The size and importance of the comic chorus continues to decrease. Performances are given not only in Athens, but in other cities and towns as well; and, as we should expect, there is a tendency to cut down on the chorus in the case of a traveling company. We hear of seven *choreutae* in a performance of comedy at Delphi in 276 B.C., and of only four *choreutae* in a comedy of the following century, on the island of Delos. This trend was accelerated by the rise in the third century of actors' and musicians' guilds, and the accompanying emphasis on contests in which individual artists, without choruses, competed for prizes.

From the latter part of the fourth century on, it was the custom to re-produce at the festivals some of the best of the comedies written earlier. Also, newly written comedies continued to be presented down to the Christian era. It seems evident that the chorus of comedy endured longer than did the chorus of tragedy. We are not sure of the date of its final disappearance; some scholars cite the second century, some the first. Probably as long as Greek comedy was performed there was in it a chorus of some sort, if only a small *kōmos*. It is interesting that the comic chorus should end on this note—for it was with a *kōmos* that Greek comedy really began.

But the dances usually associated with comedy had not vanished. Petronius, in the *Cena* (52.8) is evidence, among other Latin writers, that a form, at least, of the *kordax* was well known in the first century of the Christian era. In Greece itself, as we have seen, performances of the *kordax* in honor of Apollo are attested on the island of Amorgos in the Roman imperial period. Apollonius of Tyana, visiting the theatre in Athens during the Dionysiac festival of the Anthesteria, in the first century, found some chanting of solemn Orphic verse; but interspersed with it were dances which his biographer, Philostratus,[102] calls *lygismoi*.

---

102 Philostratus *Vit. Apoll.* 4.21.

The *lygismos,* or "writhing" figure, was, of course, a characteristic one of the ancient *kordax.* Apollonius, who had looked forward to seeing and hearing restrained and beautiful excerpts from classical drama, was horrified at what he actually observed. Far from being inappropriate to a Dionysiac festival, however, the dances which he saw would seem actually to have harked back to the spirit, at least, of early comedy. Apollonius is said to have inveighed at length against the spectacle of men, clad in flamboyant costumes, engaged in "soft and effeminate" dances to flute music, in which they portrayed Horae, Nymphs, and Bacchantes, and even winds and ships. His objection to the impersonation of female beings by men seems odd in the light of the antiquity of the custom in the drama. At any rate, in spite of the protests of Apollonius and others of his day, such performances apparently continued for some time.

This incident points up the fact that there were undoubtedly presented in Greek theatres various dancing performances apart from those in the dithyramb, tragedy, comedy, and satyr play. We have already noted that the impudent *phlyakes* plays of Magna Graecia, with their masked actors in ridiculously padded costumes, made use of some dancing. So, in all probability, did the performances of the Spartan *deikēlistai.* In like manner, the mimes, brief sketches of everyday life, apparently sometimes featured women in "strip-teases" to music, or introduced boisterous dances.

In the tenth book of the *Metamorphoses* of Apuleius (29-34) there is an extended account of a great spectacle supposedly presented in the theatre of Corinth in the second century of the Christian era. The performance began, says the author, with "funny dances" by professionals—"ludicris scaenicorum choreis." Next came a pyrrhic dance "in the Greek manner": Young boys and girls, conspicuous for their beauty and for their shining garments, in it exhibited "graceful movements, rich in gesture," "now bending into a wheeling circle, now joined into an oblique line," now in "alternating lines," "now arranged in a rectangle," now dancing individually. The pyrrhic dance was followed by an elaborate orchestic version of the legend of the judgment of Paris. The scene was a high hill made of wood, with green verdure, living trees, a flowing stream, and real goats feeding upon the grass.

[101]

Against this background the whole story was enacted with dance and gesture, by handsome dancers of both sexes. The characters portrayed were Paris, Mercury, Juno with Castor and Pollux as attendants, Minerva with Terror and Fear, Venus with a throng of small Cupids, and with Graces and Horae following after. The dances are described in some detail, as well as is the finale, in which a stream of wine poured down from the top of the hill, and the hill then descended out of sight beneath the floor. Whether this account preserves a record of a real performance, we do not know. Certainly lavish orchestic and mythological spectacles were very popular in the period of the Roman empire. Some features of the account suggest a performance in an amphitheatre rather than in a theatre. The fact that the dances were intended to be followed by a public exhibition of intercourse between Lucius (in the guise of an ass) and a woman condemned to be killed by wild beasts, and the fact that Lucius expresses the fear that a beast may be let loose without warning, and may kill him along with the woman (34), might indicate a setting in an arena. However, the author makes use in the passage of such words as *cavea, scaena, scaenici, aulaeum, siparium,* which are usually associated with the theatre.

IV

THE DANCE

OF THE

SATYR PLAY

Late in the sixth century before Christ, Pratinas of Phlius is said to have introduced at Athens a new kind of performance—the satyr play.[1] It was short, was written in verse, and was in general a burlesque presentation of a mythological theme. It was loud, noisy, even riotous, its language was by no means elevated, and it was full of obscenities. The chorus of twelve *choreutae* represented *sileni*, "horse-men," or satyrs, "goat-men," or a fusion of the two. Their leader portrayed Silenus, the elderly, fat, tipsy, snub-nosed attendant of Dionysus.[2]

At first the satyr plays seem to have been presented singly—we do not know just when during the Dionysiac festival, or where.

---

[1] The following works are helpful for an understanding of the origin and nature of the satyr drama: Margarete Bieber, *The History of the Greek and Roman Theater* (2nd ed.; Princeton, 1961); Roy C. Flickinger, *The Greek Theater and Its Drama* (4th ed.; Chicago, 1936), pp. 23-33 and *passim;* A. W. Pickard-Cambridge, *Dithyramb, Tragedy, and Comedy* (1st ed.; Oxford, 1927; 2nd ed., revised by T. B. L. Webster; New York, 1962); also, *The Dramatic Festivals of Athens* (Oxford, 1953); Ervin Roos, *Die Tragische Orchestik im Zerrbild der altattischen Komödie* (Lund, 1951); Frank Brommer, *Satyroi* (Würzburg, 1937); also, *Satyrspiele, Bilder Griechischer Vasen* (1st ed.; Berlin, 1944; 2nd ed.; 1959); Gerald F. Else, "Aristotle and Satyr Play I," *Transactions of the American Philological Association,* LXX (1939), 139-157; V. Festa, "Sikinnis," *Memorie della Reale Accademia di Archeologia,* III (1918), 2-60; cf. Suidas *s.v.* "Pratinas."

[2] As Brommer, *Satyrspiele* (1st ed.; above, note 1), pp. 32-33, points out, on vase paintings of the early fifth century youthful *sileni* appear, as contrasted with the more elderly types seen before, and eventually "families" of grandfather, father, youth, small boy, and infant *sileni* are seen, with Maenads serving as "mothers."

[103]

Soon it became the custom for each of the playwrights competing in the tragic contest at the City Dionysia to present in the theatre three tragedies and one satyr play, the latter serving as a sort of "comic relief" for the audience, after the solemnity of the tragedies. In 501 B.C. each tragic writer was required to do so.

We know the names, and something of the plots, of scores of Athenian satyr plays. But of all the plays of this type written and produced over the years, only one complete play (the *Cyclops* of Euripides), one other in an incomplete form (the *Ichneutae* of Sophocles), and brief fragments of several others, have survived.

The structure of a satyr play was in general similar to that of a tragedy: first, perhaps, a prologue; then the *parodos*, or entrance of the chorus, with an accompanying choral song, usually in strophic form; dramatic episodes or dialogues, separated by choral song and dance; and a brief *exodos*, or departure of the chorus from the *orchēstra*, with a line or two of song. During the play, it is conjectured that the chorus on occasion may have separated into two semi-choruses, as in comedy. Two or three actors seem to have been used; the *Cyclops* requires three, but two would suffice for the *Ichneutae*, if we may judge from the script as we have it.

Various writers, and particularly Brommer,[3] have endeavored to determine, from vase paintings and other representations, how a satyr play, as produced in the theatre, would look. This is admittedly a very difficult task, and many scholars have felt that no vase painting can be trusted as a factual representation of an actual performance of a satyr play—nor, indeed, of a tragedy or a comedy. Greek art, as they point out, abounds in representations of *sileni* and satyrs engaged in all sorts of activity, some of which may actually reflect a performance in the theatre, but some of which may be derived from legend, some may be a composite, and some may be merely the product of the artists' imagination.

Brommer takes the following as criteria for interpreting a given vase painting as a scene from a real satyr play: the presence of mythological characters, especially those not ordinarily associated with legends of Dionysus; a flute-player, accompanying the action; and "sileni" who are obviously men wearing masks, and

---

[3] Brommer, *Satyrspiele* (both editions; above, note 1), *passim*.

costumes with horses' tails. Brommer's conclusions, though not always compelling, are interesting. In one respect, at least, his findings agree with those of many other writers—i.e., in the matter of the interpretation of the famous Pronomos vase in Naples, dating from about 400 B.C.,[4] as a portrayal of a troupe about to stage a satyr play.[5]

Since the plots of the satyr play, like most of the plots of tragedy, dealt with mythological themes, we should expect that the costumes worn by the actors representing the major characters would resemble those worn in tragedy. On the Pronomos vase, three figures, usually identified as actors, wear elaborate garments, long-sleeved and ornately figured. There is no indication of high-soled shoes. Each actor carries a mask emphasizing the character he is to portray; the characters are customarily identified as Hesione, Heracles, and Laomedon. The central figure, Pronomos the flute-player, is richly garbed in a long, beautifully figured robe; he wears a wreath, and plays on his double flute. A young man carrying a lyre also appears in the group, and, on the other side, an extra lyre rests against the wall. The costumes of Silenus and the members of the chorus are distinctive. The man representing Silenus wears a shaggy garment suggesting an animal-skin, and over his shoulder is the hide of a panther.[6] The members of the chorus wear or carry masks. They show the scanty costume which became standardized for the satyric chorus in fourth-century Athens: trunks or shorts, here shaggy and resembling a goat-skin, but usually apparently made of ordinary cloth; a conspicuous phallus; and a horse's tail attached to the trunks. They appear unshod, but it is generally believed that the *choreutae* actually wore soft shoes, perhaps even designed in imitation of horse's hoofs. Flickinger and others have recognized the costumes of the *choreutae*

---

[4] See also Pickard-Cambridge, *Dithyramb* (1st ed.; above, note 1), Fig. 11, facing p. 152; (2nd ed.; above, note 1), Pl. XIII; Fritz Weege, *Der Tanz in der Antike* (Halle/Saale, 1926), Abb. 161, p. 117; Flickinger (above, note 1), p. 25; Louis Séchan, *La danse grecque antique* (Paris, 1930), Plate XI, p. 204.

[5] Pickard-Cambridge, *Dramatic Festivals* (above, note 1), Fig. 28 and p. 180, with his n. 1, regards the scene rather as "Dionysus in the midst of his *thiasos*, embracing both his satyrs and tragedy." He says that the three distinctive figures are not "actors dressing up," but members of the imaginary *thiasos*, "characters in a recently victorious play."

[6] Cf. Pollux 4.118.

on this vase as in reality a composite of the garb of the Ionian *sileni*, or horse-men, and the Dorian satyrs, or goat-men, of early Dionysiac ritual.[7] In its brevity, it is a costume eminently suited to the lively role of the chorus in the satyr drama.

The dance played a very important part in the satyr play. This is as we should expect. Not only did the satyr drama as a genre have its roots in Dionysiac dances, but we know that Pratinas, its "inventor," made extensive use of the dance in his plays. Athenaeus indeed lists him (1.22 A) with the early playwrights who were called *orchēstai*, "dancers," because they used the dance a great deal in their dramas, and also "apart from their own poems, taught those wishing to dance." In other words, he was a dancing teacher as well as a playwright, and he very probably invented *schēmata* for his own plays, as many of his contemporaries did for their tragedies.

Like other types of dramatic dance, the dance of the "satyrs" was in general performed to the music of the double flute. Several Greek writers tell us that the satyric dance was of a distinctive character and had a special name—*sikinnis*.[8] The Suidas *Lexicon* (*s.v.* "sikinnis") states that there was an alternative form of the name—*sikinnon*. The "satyrs" when performing the dance were called *sikinnistai*.[9] In addition, we are informed[10] that there was a type of flute music called the *sikinnotyrbē*, and that it regularly accompanied a dance; obviously the dance in question would be the *sikinnis*. We are told also that the *sikinnotyrbē* was "a kind of flute, a kind of song, and a kind of dance."[11] Oddly enough, the word *sikinnotyrbē* combines *sikinnis* with *tyrbē*, "rout, revel"— which is related to *tyrbasia*, the name of the characteristic dance of the dithyramb. Since both dithyramb and satyr play were of Dionysiac origin, it is likely that the dance of the latter may have

7 See Flickinger (above, note 1), pp. 24-32 and 341; Brommer, *Satyrspiele* (1st ed.; above, note 1), p. 11.

8 Pollux 4.99; Athenaeus 1.20 E; 14.630 B, C; schol. Aristophanes *Clouds* 540; Dionysius Hal. 7.72.12; Hesychius *s.v.*; schol. AB *Iliad* 16.617; *Et. Mag.* 635.1, *s.v.* "*orchēstai*" and 712.54-59, *s.v.* "sikinnis"; Lucian *Salt.* 26. Johannes Meursius, in "*Orchestra*," in Jacobus Gronovius' *Thesaurus Graecarum Antiquitatum* (Venice, 1732-1737), VIII, *s.v.* "sikinnis," assembles the most important Greek references to this dance.

9 Athenaeus 1.20 E; 14.630 B.

10 Athenaeus 14.618 C.

11 Meursius (above, note 8), *s.v.* "sikinnotyrbē."

borne a considerable resemblance to that of the primitive form of the dithyramb.

The Greeks indulged in a great deal of speculation as to the "inventor" and place of origin of various forms of the dance. Much of this speculation is highly imaginative; and on the source of the dance of the satyr play ancient conjecture runs rampant. One of the reputed "inventors" of the *sikinnis* is a Sikanos, usually identified as an early king of Athens; but some scholars think that Sikanos, king of the Sicilians, is referred to, and that in the legend the *sikinnis* is confused with the iambic choruses of the Sicilians.[12] Another man credited with the invention is a "barbarian" or a Cretan named Sikinnos.[13] Still others are Sikinnos or Sikanos, a "Persian captive" of Themistocles, and a certain man named Thersippus.[14] Even more fanciful are derivations from the name of "one of the satyrs of mythology," and from the name of Sikinnis, a Nymph attendant upon the goddess Cybele.[15] The author of the latter suggestion does add one significant comment: "They say," he remarks, "that the Phrygians first danced the *sikinnis* in honor of Dionysus Sabazius." It is known that the cult of Dionysus was an important one among the Phrygians and the Thracians, and that in many respects it resembled the cult of Sabazius.

Other ancient conjectures as to the origin and significance of the name of the dance are: that it is derived from *kineisthai*, "move," *kinēsis*, "movement"; or that it comes from *seiesthai*, "move violently, shake."[16] Both these explanations are inadmissible etymologically. Modern scholarship[17] tends to regard the word *sikinnis* as of Thraco-Phrygian origin, from a root meaning "leap, dance, move with agility." Thus it is possible that the *sikinnis* may indeed have had its roots in Asia Minor. Some writers, however, have seen the dance as stemming from a purely Greek apotropaic and fertility rite.[18]

---

12 *Et. Mag.* 712.54-59, *s.v.* "sikinnis."

13 Athenaeus 1.20 E; 14.630 B.

14 Plutarch *Themist.* 12.3-4; *Et. Mag.* 712.54-59, *s.v.* "sikinnis"; Athenaeus 14.630 B.

15 Lucian *Salt.* 22; Eustathius *Iliad* 1078.20.

16 Athenaeus 14.630 B-C; *Et. Mag.* and Hesychius *s.v.* "sikinnis."

17 Cf. Émile Boisacq, *Dictionnaire étymologique de la langue grecque* (4th ed.; Heidelberg, 1950), pp. 864 and 447.

18 Cf. Séchan (above, note 4), p. 214.

Not to be overlooked here is the fact that some, at least, of the ancient commentators connect the *sikinnis* with Crete, and in particular with the dance of the Curetes,[19] the ritual dancers who leaped high, clashing spear on shield as did their mythological counterparts to protect the divine child, Zeus, after his birth in a Cretan cave. This dance is generally regarded as an apotropaic and fertility charm.[20] In this connection probably must be considered the statement in the Hesychius *Lexicon* (*s.v.* "sikinnis") that the *sikinnis* was *stratiōtikē*, "military," and *syntonos*, "violent," and also the remark in the *Etymologicum Magnum* and elsewhere[21] that the *sikinnis* was *hieratikē*, "priestly." The Cretans reached great heights in the art of the dance, and in fact were regarded by the Greeks as the "inventors" of that art. Many of the dances of the Greeks seem to go back to prehistoric Crete. It is entirely possible that the *sikinnis* may have reached the Greeks from Asia Minor by way of the Minoans and Mycenaeans.[22] Several of the features of the Dionysiac cult find their counterpart in the rituals of Crete—particularly in connection with the divine child. The apparently great difference between a chorus of "horse-men" or "goat-men" in a Greek satyr play and a chorus of armed warriors in a Minoan ritual is not so significant as would appear at first glance, for the Curetes were probably not always armed, and were originally rather "noise-making" dancers than warriors.[23]

All our sources of information agree that the *sikinnis* was lively, rapid, vigorous, and lewd.[24] It made use of expressive gestures, many of them obscene. It seems to have burlesqued more serious dances with audacious impertinence.[25] It abounded in noise, buffoonery, "horse-play," and acrobatics, sometimes of a startling na-

---

[19] Cf. Athenaeus 1.20 E; 14.630 B; Strabo 10.3.7.11-12.

[20] Cf. Lillian B. Lawler, "The Dance in Ancient Crete," *Studies Presented to David M. Robinson* (St. Louis, 1951), I, 23-51 and especially 24-28.

[21] *Et. Mag.* 635.1-2, *s.v.* "orchēstai"; schol. AB *Iliad* 16.617.

[22] Kurt Latte, *De Saltationibus Gracecorum Capita Quinque* (Giessen, 1913), pp. 89-90, thinks that the Greeks obtained the *sikinnis* ultimately from the Minoan Cretans, and transferred the dance to the cult of Dionysus.

[23] Lawler (above, note 20).

[24] Athenaeus 14.630 B, C; *Et. Mag. s.v.* "tragoedia," 768-772. The latter source, in stating (764) that the tragic choruses sometimes used "*schēmata* of goats," evidently confuses tragedy and the satyr play.

[25] Cf. Dionysius Hal. 7.72.10-12.

ture. In many respects it would probably remind us of the antics of our circus clowns—but with an accompanying licentiousness which could have no place on any modern stage.

There is one passage in Athenaeus, however (14.629 D), which has somewhat complicated our understanding of the general nature of the *sikinnis*. The writer introduces a list of names of dances, most of them generic in type, with the statement that they are all *stasimōtera* and *poikilōtera*, and that they have a *haplousteran* form of choreography. These adjectives are all in the comparative degree. Whether they imply a comparison with dances mentioned in the preceding section, or are to be interpreted not as true comparatives but as denoting "rather," "somewhat," etc., is not at once evident. The list is as follows: "daktyloi iambikē Molossikē emmeleia kordax sikinnis Persikē Phrygios nibatismos Thrakios kalabrismos telesias"—with the added comment that the latter is the same dance as the *Makedonikē*. Here many problems arise. Does the word *Persikē*, "Persian," for instance, go with *sikinnis*, or is it the name of a separate dance? Was there perhaps a "Persian *sikinnis*," as distinguished from the true or Greek *sikinnis*? Or is Athenaeus here speaking of the same dance which he himself, quoting Xenophon (*Anab.* 6.1.10) speaks of elsewhere (1.16 A) as *to Persikon*? This is the dance which is associated with the *oklasma*. It is characterized by Xenophon as one in which the dancer, carrying two shields, clashes them together as he performs a "knee-dance," crouching and then rising, in a manner which recalls to the modern reader a characteristic Russian folk-dance.

We note also that in Athenaeus' list the *emmeleia* is preceded by the adjective *Molossikē*, "Molossic"; again, we are not sure whether the adjective is to be taken with the noun ("the Molossic *emmeleia*"), or whether the author is listing two dances, a "Molossic dance" and the *emmeleia*. A priori, in this vexed passage it would seem likely that *Molossikē* is to be separated from *emmeleia* and taken as a third dance, together with the two preceding ones evidently named for their rhythm—*daktyloi* and *iambikē;* that next are to be taken the three dances of the theatre—*emmeleia, kordax,* and *sikinnis;* and that finally the *Persikē* is to be taken with the Phrygian, Thracian, and Macedonian national dances following.

Now we return to the adjectives applied by Athenaeus to the whole group of dances here listed. Again we encounter difficul-

[109]

ties—and this time even apparent contradictions. *Stasimos* might mean "stable, steady, stationary, regular, set"—but *poikilos* may denote "unstable, variegated, diverse, changing, manifold, colorful"! *Haplous* definitely means "simple, plain." If a comparison is implied with the preceding section, it must be with the *apokinos*, *maktrismos*, and similar lewd dances; but these, as we have seen, are commonly associated with the *kordax*—and the *kordax* is one of the dances in our list! Accordingly, I believe we must rule out an implied comparison with the dances previously mentioned. I should suggest that Athenaeus' meaning is that the dances listed in this passage are "rather definite in form," are "rather colorful," and possess "a somewhat simple choreography." These statements do actually apply to all the dances which he then lists. If they seem slightly vague to the modern reader, it is well to bear in mind that Athenaeus could not possibly have seen any of the dances here mentioned, since they flourished at a much earlier period, and had by his time already passed into oblivion.

What do we know specifically of the choreography, steps, figures, and gestures of the dance of the satyr play? Not as much as we should like to know, certainly. However, our various sources, and in particular the two extant satyr plays, do contribute some information.

In a study of the plays, one must observe great caution when making deductions with reference to the *sikinnis*. Just as in comedy not all the dancing represents the *kordax*, so in the satyr play there must have been dances of types other than the *sikinnis*.

If we may judge from the two plays which have come down to us, apparently the satyric *choreutae* did not enter the *orchēstra* in the formal "tetragonal" arrangement which is attested for tragedy, and which was perhaps frequently used in comedy as well. In the *Cyclops* of Euripides members of the chorus enter with considerable freedom of movement, driving and dragging real or imaginary sheep and goats with them. Lest we be tempted to regard the entrance as not properly an exhibition of dancing, Silenus speaks of the *choreutae* as actually dancing—and dancing the *sikinnis*, at that (37). It is interesting that Silenus, in describing their entrance, uses the participle *sauloumenoi* (40) of their gait. This word implies an affected, mincing walk with exaggerated movements of the hips, usually associated with the *kor-*

dax, the dance of comedy.[26] Arrived in the center of the *orchēstra*, the *choreutae* continue, in the midst of lines honoring Aphrodite and Dionysus, to struggle with the goats throughout the *parodos*. If these lines do indeed accompany the *sikinnis*, we may infer that that dance did not require uniform movements on the part of the dancers, but permitted them to dance (or cavort!) as individuals.

The text of the *Ichneutae* of Sophocles is much more mutilated than is that of the *Cyclops* of Euripides. However, it is quite evident that in the *parodos* of the former play (lines 57-70),[27] the *choreutae* enter in their appropriate guise of *ichneutai*, "trackers," seeking under the urging of their leader for some trace of the lost cattle of Apollo. Walton[28] sees in the play evidence that the equine satyrs here are "made up" and act "as if they are a pack of hunting dogs" (cf. lines 85-89, 223-226). Such burlesque combinations, he points out, are not unknown in the Greek drama. Whether Walton is correct in his hypothesis or not, certainly the entrance of the chorus in this play would not seem to be in tetragonal formation.

Again, the departure of the chorus at the end of the *Cyclops* gives no hint of any distinctive formation. In the two final lines (708-709) the *choreutae* merely state their intention of sailing away with Odysseus, and of serving Dionysus in the future. The conclusion of the *Ichneutae* is lost.

One of the most interesting passages in the *Ichneutae* is the choral ode in lines 170-198, together with the four preceding lines (166-169), with which Silenus introduces the ode. After telling the members of the chorus that he will call them by whistling at them, as if they were dogs (cf. Walton's theory here), Silenus says: ". . . all' hei' [a]phistō trizygēs hoimou basin." Walker[29] sees here a reference to a parody of military tactics, executed to the music of

---

[26] Here we may compare a passage in Lucian (*Dionys.* 1), in which the author describes young rustics, votaries of Dionysus, as dancing the *kordax* in his honor, "naked, and wearing horns and tails."

[27] A. C. Pearson, *The Fragments of Sophocles* (Cambridge, 1917), I. Citations from the *Ichneutae* in this chapter are from Pearson's edition, unless otherwise indicated.

[28] Francis R. Walton, "A Problem in the *Ichneutae* of Sophocles," *Harvard Studies in Classical Philology*, XLVI (1935), 167-189.

[29] Richard J. Walker, *The Ichneutae of Sophocles* (London, 1919), pp. 177, 184, 527.

a military march, played on the flute, in the type of music known as the *polemikon*, "warlike."[30] We may recall in this connection that the Hesychius *Lexicon* (*s.v.* "sikinnis") states that the *sikinnis* was "spirited," and was—or perhaps we should understand *could be*, at times—*stratiōtikē*, "military," probably in burlesque fashion. Walker translates the line, "Up, now, set your feet to go forward in three bands under one yoke," and explains it (p. 527) as meaning "in a formation of three single-files." This he interprets as referring to a small *lochos*, or company, of twelve soldiers divided into three sets of four men each, for reconnoitering in the woods. He is obviously thinking also of the use of *zyga* to denote the ranks of *choreutae* in the tragic chorus. If he is right, it is possible that here, if anywhere in the extant satyr plays, we may have a dance formation, if only in burlesque, which suggests the rectangular alignment of the tragic chorus. Pearson, however, regards the line as referring to a metaphorical "leaving of the cross-roads"—i.e., "hesitating no longer" (pp. 248-249). So vexed is the passage!

There ensues the choral passage which begins with the strange line (170): "Hu, hu, hu, ps, ps, a, a, tell what you're worried about!" Some scholars think the odd syllables or sounds may represent animal noises. Pearson thinks they may represent a drover's cry. The rest of the ode sounds oddly irrelevant to the play —except, perhaps, lines 194-196, which seem to urge the group back into position after some wandering afield.

Very striking in the *Ichneutae* are also lines 204-214. Here the chorus and Silenus have reached the house of Cyllene, and Silenus (or the *coryphaeus*) apparently calls to the master of the household to open the door (204-210). There is no response. Thereupon the speaker cries out (211-214) that he will compel the householder to hear him, even though he may be deaf, by his "swift leaps and kicks"—*pēdēmata kraipna* and *laktismata*. Evidently he and the accompanying satyrs proceed to suit the action to the word. Instead of a man, Cyllene appears from the house. She asks why the group has come "with so much loud shouting" (216), and so much "kicking of the feet" (231). She says that she has been frightened by the wild uproar (231-236).

---

[30] Athenaeus 14.618 C.

There are doubtful readings in the passage, and there have been differing interpretations of the lines. Walker[31] cannot understand how Silenus, merely by leaping and kicking the ground, could possibly produce a noise greater than the preceding song of the chorus, and so loud that even a deaf householder would be able to hear it. Accordingly, he believes that Silenus kicked at the front door. One need hardly point out, however, that the whole chorus seems to have joined in, with accompanying yells. If *rhyth-mōn* is the correct reading in line 232, the action is a real dance. We have here leaps, kicks, stamping, noise, a swift tempo—a combination which points directly to the *sikinnis*. Walker thinks the action was accompanied by the type of flute music known as "door-striking"—*thyrokopikon* or *krousithyron*.[32]

There must have been a close similarity between the *sikinnis* and Bacchic revel-dances. That this was indeed so is seen in the *Cyclops*. There Silenus (37-40), just before the members of the chorus enter, apparently dancing the *sikinnis*, likens their progress to the *kōmoi*, accompanied by the lyre, with which they had in former days escorted the young Dionysus to the dwelling of Althaea. Later, in the choral ode in lines 483-510, during which the drunken Cyclops enters, there is a brief *kōmos* (495-502), with praise of love and wine. The Cyclops seems to dance with the *choreutae* at this point,[33] in clumsy, uncouth, drunken capering. A few lines farther along (520-523), the *choreutae* sing longingly of ivy-crowned Dionysus, and probably dance a few steps in his honor. On the other hand, Polyphemus, at his entrance at line 203, had called the satyrs to their duties, saying that "Dionysus is not here," nor Bacchic revels, nor bronze *krotala*, nor the rolling of hand-drums (204-205). The same note had been struck in lines 25, 63-81. In like manner in the *Ichneutae* (215-222) Cyllene contrasts the present activity of the satyrs with their reveling in Dionysus' train, along with the Nymphs, in former days.

Similar to the revel-dances of the chorus in the *Cyclops* is a dance by Silenus, at lines 156-157 in the same play. Previously Odysseus has asked (123) Silenus if the local inhabitants make wine. Silenus replies (124), "Not at all! For they dwell in a dance-

---

[31] Walker (above, note 29), pp. 36 and 184.
[32] Walker (above, note 29), p. 184; cf. Athenaeus 14.618 C.
[33] Cf. Theocritus 7.151-153 and schol. ad loc.

less land!"—thereby making the customary association of wine and the dance. As soon as Silenus drinks of the wine proffered by Odysseus, he exclaims in joy (156-157) that Dionysus bids him dance. Evidently at this point he does perform a solo dance. Later (171-172) Silenus extols the dance "that makes one forget his troubles."

Walker sees in the lines numbered 403-405 and 408-410 of his edition of the *Ichneutae* a *kallinikos*, a choral dance of victory.[34] However, the choral ode survives in so mutilated a condition that it is impossible to determine the nature of the accompanying dance. Certainly the ode is in general expressive of the satyrs' joy at accomplishing their mission, and it includes an invocation of Apollo, who then (411) appears.

The *Cyclops* contains two brief choral odes which may have been accompanied by burlesque dances. The first of these, lines 511-518, is a mock *epithalamium*, or wedding-song. To be sure, the passage is grimly metaphorical, and refers by inference to the coming blinding of the Cyclops by the "bridal torch." Yet to it the chorus may have executed a brief processional dance suggestive of, or a burlesque of, a wedding procession. The second ode, lines 655-662, is sung by the chorus in response to Odysseus' request (653-654) that they voice some encouragement to him and his men in their grim task of burning out the Cyclops' eye. The ode proper, beginning at line 657, has something of the flavor of an incantation, and may have been accompanied by a brief burlesque dance.

There is evidence in both the satyr plays for various steps and *schēmata* which seem distinctive. We have already noted a reference to one step or gait used in the satyr play—that described by the participle *sauloumenoi* (*Cyclops* 40). References to *schēmata* are numerous.

Outstanding among the *schēmata* regarded by the ancients as characteristic of the satyr play is the "peering" *schēma*,[35] which is found in tragedy and comedy as well, although apparently

---

[34] Walker (above, note 29), p. 184; cf. Lillian B. Lawler, *"Orchēsis Kallinikos," Transactions of the American Philological Association*, LXXIX (1948), 254-267.
[35] Photius *s.vv.* "skopos," "skōpeuma"; cf. Cl. Salmasius, in *Historiae Augustae Scriptores Sex* (Lugduni Batavorum, 1671), II, 835-836.

THE DANCE OF THE SATYR PLAY

less frequently. By the Greeks the *schēma* was usually called *skopos* or *hyposkopos cheir*. By an odd etymological confusion of *skopos* and *skōps*, the word for "owl," the *schēma* was associated in antiquity with various owl dances, and as a result it was sometimes called "the owl-*schēma*"—*skōpeuma, skōps,* or even *skōpos*.[36] This confusion was undoubtedly strengthened by the fact that owls do gaze fixedly and twist and turn their heads in the attempt to see in the daylight. The peering *schēma* is associated also with the artistic type of the divine shepherd, Pan,[37] as *aposkopos* or *aposkopeuōn*, shielding his eyes with his hand and peering out to look for his herd, or for signs of enemies or storms. Pan, as we know, passes into association with Dionysus, and soon in Greek art Pans, satyrs, and *sileni* appear together in Dionysiac routs.

Elsewhere I have suggested[38] that one of the commonplaces of plot in the satyr play was the motif of searching, seeking, peering. At the beginning of the *Cyclops*, Silenus tells us that he and his satyrs had been searching for Dionysus when they were shipwrecked on the coast of Polyphemus' domain. The motif of searching and peering (and, of course, much emphasis upon eyes and seeing) is evident throughout the play—as, e.g., at lines 36-37, 85, and 193. It is possible that some adaptation of the *schēma* of the *skopos* is to be seen also in lines 211-213. Here Polyphemus, roaring at the satyrs for not performing their duties as he thinks they should, bids them peremptorily "Look up and not down!" They reply eagerly, "Just see, we have raised our heads up to Zeus himself, and we are looking at the stars and Orion!" There must have been amusing byplay connected with the "looking up at the stars."

The whole plot of the *Ichneutae* of Sophocles, and, indeed the very title itself, is concerned with searching. In this play the *ichneutai*, or "trackers," are the members of the chorus, who seek persistently for, and find, the lost cattle of Apollo and the baby Hermes who has stolen them. Throughout the play, references to peering and searching, and actual use of the verb *skopeō* and its derivatives, abound. We may note the following examples: Used

---

[36] Cf. Lillian B. Lawler, "The Dance of the Owl," *Transactions of the American Philological Association*, LXX (1939), 482-502.

[37] Cf. Photius *s.vv.* "Panos skōlos," "Panos skopos," "skopos." Also, Hesychius *s.vv.* "Panos (s)kōlon."

[38] Lawler, "Owl" (above, note 36), 500-501.

[115]

by Apollo, line 7; used by Silenus, chiefly in bidding the chorus search for the cattle, lines 46, 124, 158, and probably 85; used by the chorus, lines 57-70, 92-102, 106-108, 109-116, 200.

Fragments of other satyr plays which have been preserved contain similar allusions to peering and searching.[39]

Not all the references which we have noted are to passages in which dancing in the modern sense of the word is engaged in. However, as we have observed frequently, *cheironomia*, or interpretative gesturing, was regarded as an aspect of the dance; and such gesturing accompanied even dialogue in a Greek play.[40] Any of the passages cited above might be accompanied by "peering" gestures; those which occur in choral odes might reasonably be expected to be associated with the *schēma* of the *skopos*.

In the *Ichneutae* there is a curious passage (118-124) in which Silenus expostulates with the *choreutae* for searching "bent over towards the earth," like hedgehogs or monkeys. Much has been written on the lines. Walker[41] thinks that the crouching posture of the satyrs here mentioned is due to their "agony of terror." It is true that Silenus asks them what they are afraid of (126), and the satyrs do show fear at the loud noise of the newly-invented lyre, which they soon hear (cf. 136-145). But it would seem much more likely that their posture referred to in lines 118-124 is rather an exaggerated *skopos* or peering, searching *schēma* than a manifestation of prostrate fear. Earlier (85-90) Silenus had specifically bidden them search "bending over double," guided by scent. Incidentally, both Suidas and Photius, in defining the word *rhiknousthai (s.v.)*, mention its use in the dance, and refer to the *Ichneutae*. As we have seen, *rhiknousthai* is attested as the name of a lewd *schēma* of the dance of comedy, in which the dancer bent over and rotated his hips. It is possible that at this point in the *Ichneutae*, the satyrs, while bent over, may have interpolated a few wriggles like those of the characteristic dance of comedy!

There seems on occasion to have been a related *schēma* of "listening," probably with exaggerated pantomime, in the choral odes of the satyr play. Passages in the *Ichneutae* in which the

[39] Lawler, "Owl" (above, note 36), 501-502.
[40] Athenaeus 1.21 F, 22 A; schol. Aristophanes *Clouds* 1352; Suidas *s.v.* "emmeleia"; cf. Plato *Laws* 7.816 A; *Rep.* 3.396 A-397 B.
[41] Walker (above, note 29), p. 518.

[116]

choreutae may have used this *schēma* are lines 107-110; 130-138; and 198; and, in the *Cyclops*, such lines as 488-491.

The lexicographer Pollux, listing various types of dancing and dancers (4.104), speaks of "satyrs dancing *hypotroma*." Whether he is referring to the *sikinnis* or not we do not know; but a *schēma* or dance of this name would fit in quite logically with the *sikinnis*. The word *hypotroma* is the neuter plural of the adjective *hypotromos*, which means "trembling, quivering, shaking." We recall that one ancient explanation of the word *sikinnis* was that it was derived from *seiesthai*, "to shake"[42]—an impossible etymology, but an interesting one in this connection. A *schēma* known as *hypotroma* in a satyric dance might imply either a lewd shaking (as seen in many primitive fertility dances even to this day) or an exaggerated trembling or quaking inspired by fear. Both could occur in either of the two satyr plays which have come down to us. In particular, their dread of Polyphemus furnishes ample opportunity for the display of fear on the part of the *choreutae* in the *Cyclops*—especially at lines 203-213, 635-641. In the *Ichneutae*, the terror of the satyrs at the strange sounds which they hear—as, e.g., at lines 130-138, 155-159, and 254-255—would give occasion for the use of the *schēma*.

Other *schēmata* customarily listed as satyric include the *strobilos*, "whirling" (Athenaeus 14.630 A); the *konisalos* (Hesychius, *s.v.*), a spirited leaping with exposure of the genitals; other leaps, *skirtēmata*, of various kinds (Lucian *Bacch.* 5); *podos diarrhipha* (Athenaeus 14.617 F), a "flinging of the foot"; the *sobas* or *sobein* (Athenaeus 14.629 F), which Festa[43] interpreted as "violent turning on one's own axis," but which others regard merely as "violent, driving motion"; and the *knismos* or "the itch."[44] The *schēma* called *skelos rhiptein*,[45] usually regarded as "a high kick," was interpreted by Festa[46] as the lively figure portrayed often on vase paintings, in which a dancing satyr raises one leg sharply to the side, at hip height, with the knee bent, and the foot pointing down—and then, presumably, raises the other leg to a similar posi-

---

[42] *Et. Mag.* and Hesychius *s.v.* "sikinnis."
[43] Festa (above, note 1), p. 58.
[44] Pollux 4.100; Athenaeus 14.618 C.
[45] Schol. Aristophanes *Wasps* 1530; cf. *Peace* 332.
[46] Festa (above, note 1), pp. 66-68.

tion immediately thereafter. On the other hand, Roos[47] thinks these vase paintings rather portray the *podos diarrhipha*.

Some scholars see in obscure lexicographical passages[48] an indication of a *schēma* called *Panos skōlon, Panos kōlon,* or *Panos skōlos,* which they interpret variously as "Pan's leg," "Pan's thorn," or "Pan's pointed stick," and in which the dancer was beaten over the legs. However, the references adduced may be merely corruptions of *skopos,* the peering *schēma* often associated with the shepherd-god Pan.

Among the *schēmata* attested as "tragika", there are several which are apparently common to tragedy and the satyr play. Many of these were obviously used in one or both of the plays which we have been examining. We may instance the following:

The *schēma* known as *simē cheir,* "the snub-nosed hand," in which the dancer holds the hand in such a way that the fingers curve back tensely from the palm, is frequently used as a gesture of warding off something—either something physical, or a horrible thought or sight—from the dancer's face or eyes. In these cases the hand is held before the face, palm out, the fingers curving back strongly. The *schēma* would have a place, e.g., in the *Cyclops,* in the choral ode of lines 356-374, where the horrors of Polyphemus' cannibalism are dwelt upon; during Odysseus' long recital (382-436) of the killing of some of his men; and perhaps during the Cyclops' roaring wine song (503-510). In the *Ichneutae* it might be used in various passages indicating fear—as, e.g., in lines 130-138. Other connotations of the gesture, as we have seen them in the dance of tragedy, would also have a place in the satyr plays.

The *schēma* of the sword-thrust, *xiphismos,* or, by extension, of the thrusting of any sharp weapon, would have abundant use in the *Cyclops.* It might, for example, accompany Silenus' account (lines 7-8) of how he slew Enceladus with a spear; or the vivid lines in which Odysseus (457-459) and the chorus (483-486) tell how the stake is to be driven into the Cyclops' eye. The *schēma* undoubtedly came, in time, to have an obscene significance. In that connotation it might find an appropriate place anywhere in the true *sikinnis.*

---

[47] Roos (above, note 1), p. 178.
[48] Hesychius *s.v.* "Panos (s)kōlon"; Photius *s.v.* "Panos skōlos."

The *schēma* called by the Greeks *xylou paralēpsis*, interpreted in our discussion of the tragic dance as a real or symbolic taking up or using of a wooden club or staff in mimetic enactment of beating or threatened violence, might have been used very effectively in the *Cyclops*. Polyphemus, finding the satyrs neglecting their duties, shouts at them and actually threatens them with a stick *xylō* (210-211). Whether he makes use of a real or an imaginary club at this point, the gesture would be the same. A little later (237) Silenus, relaying to the Cyclops with spirited detail an imaginary threat on the part of Odysseus, probably displays a similar gesture in mentioning the use of a whip, *mastigi*.

We have noted above the evidence for a *schēma* of "rowing" in the dance of tragedy. That a similar *schēma* or gesture may have been used on occasion in the satyr play might be indicated by the marked mention of oars in such passages as *Cyclops* 14-17 and 466-468.

Gestures and *schēmata* of supplication and prayer undoubtedly appeared in the satyr play as well as in tragedy. In the *Cyclops* there would be opportunity for such gestures and *schēmata* at lines 300, 350, 353-355, 599-600, 601, 605.

We have discussed above the *schēma* of the basket, *kalathiskos*, attested by Pollux (4.105) as "tragic," and included by Athenaeus (14.630 A) among other *schēmata* generally termed "tragic" by Greek writers. We have suggested that it may actually have had a limited use in tragedy, in plays in which members of the chorus carried baskets on their heads, or referred in choral passages to the carrying of such baskets. We have suggested also that the *schēma* may have been used in comedy, as a burlesque of the basket dances of cult ritual. A similar use in the satyr play would be entirely possible. We have already noted the fact that at times the lexicographers seem to use the adjective *tragikos* to refer to dances of the "goat-men" or satyrs.

Other *schēmata* which are called "tragika" by Greek writers, or are mentioned in a context which would imply that designation, but which by their very nature may be assumed to have been used in the satyr play as well as in tragedy are: *cheir kataprēnēs*, the slap (Athenaeus 14.630 A; Pollux 4.105), directed at either the dancer himself or another person; the *hekateris, hekaterides*, or *hekaterein*, rapid slapping or kicking, in a definite rhythm, with

[119]

alternating right and left hands or feet;[49] the *kybistēsis*, tumbling, acrobatics to music (Pollux 4.105); the *thermaustris* or *thermaustrides*, "fire-tongs," characterized by violent leaps and crossing of the feet in the air;[50] the "split," *schistās helkein* or *schisma*;[51] and probably the whirling *deinos* or *dinos* (Athenaeus 11.467 F).

Not only tragedy, but comedy also, on occasion, apparently contributed *schēmata* to the satyr play.[52] Lucian seems to say (*Salt.* 26) that in his day, at least, the *kordax* of comedy was supplemented at times by the *sikinnis;* evidently the converse also was true. We have noted a use of *sauloumenoi* in the *Cyclops* (40) and a possible use of *rhiknousthai* in the *Ichneutae* (118-124)— both *schēmata* of the dance of comedy. Another example may be some sort of "gobbling" *schēma*. Strabo (10.3.11.468) says that the Cretan dance of the Curetes included a mimetic portrayal of the swallowing of his children by Cronus. In the late Greco-Roman pantomimic dance we have a reference to a performance on the same theme, called the *Kronou teknophagia* (Lucian, *Salt.* 80) and to others portraying "the misfortunes of Thyestes" and the Tantalus-Pelops story (Lucian *Salt.* 54). Food-stealing and eating motifs are common in Athenian and Dorian comedy. In the *Birds* of Aristophanes, a "gobbling" *schēma* seems hinted at.[53] In the *Cyclops* of Euripides there is much mention of devouring—e.g., in lines 233 and 356-374. Obviously these lines would be accompanied with exaggerated gestures and *schēmata*.

We have already discussed the boisterous dances featured in the concluding lines of the *Wasps* of Aristophanes—dances which appear in comedy, are said to be dances of tragedy, and resemble in many respects the dance of the satyr play. Festa and others have identified them with the *sikinnis*.[54] Roos[55] believes they were ultimately dances of courtesans. They contain *schēmata* of "knocking at the door," of snorting, of lunging, of crouching, of high

---

49 Pollux 4.102; Athenaeus 14.630 A; Hesychius *s.v.* "hekaterein."
50 Pollux 4.102 and 105; Athenaeus 14.629 E, 630 A; Hesychius, *s.v.;* Eustathius 1601.27.
51 Pollux 4.105; Hesychius *s.v.* "schisma."
52 Cf. Eustathius 1078.20.
53 Cf. Lillian B. Lawler, "Four Dancers in the *Birds* of Aristophanes," *Transactions of the American Philological Association*, LXXIII (1942), 58-63.
54 See Roos (above, note 1), pp. 167-169.
55 Roos (above, note 1), *passim*, and especially 201-202.

kicking, of spin-turning, of leaping, of whirling a limb in its socket, of slapping, of contortions of the body. It seems highly likely that these *schēmata* were used in both the *kordax* and the *sikinnis*.

Walker[56] believes that the *Ichneutae* ended with "a grand choric finale in which the pipe and the lyre both played their parts." He bases this theory on the importance of the invention of the lyre in the plot of the play. He conjectures (page 186) that this *synaulia*[57] was the first in Athenian dramatic history, and that it may have taken the form of alternate dances (probably without song) by semi-choruses, the one to the old-fashioned flute, the other to the newer (for the drama) lyre (pages 182, 188). However, since the end of the play is entirely lost, this hypothesis of Walker's remains incapable of proof. The Pronomos vase,[58] the painted decoration on which most scholars regard as representing a preparation for a performance of a satyr play, shows one flute and two lyres.

We have scrutinized the two extant satyr plays closely for first-hand information on the nature of the dance and gestures in those plays. Of the many other satyr plays known to have been produced in the Attic theatre, we possess fragments of the text of a large number, and the titles of a great many more. However, even the most searching examination of these remnants yields virtually nothing not already known or conjectured concerning the dance of the satyr play.

Many scholars have turned to archaeological sources for additional information on the subject. Dancing satyrs and *sileni* were popular subjects among Attic vase painters, and sculptors as well, though to a lesser degree. In making use of these portrayals of the dance, the student must use the utmost caution. The fact remains that, despite innumerable conjectures, we have in art no sure portrayal of any dance of the ancient theatre. The student must bear in mind constantly that (1) any artist uses his imagination, and readily departs from documentary accuracy when he desires to do so for artistic effect; (2) the postures of figures on vases, in particular, are subject to the exigencies of space and to the canon of certain very definite artistic conventions; (3) there are dangers inherent in the assumption that a given vase painting depicts

---

56 Walker (above, note 29), p. 182.
57 Cf. Athenaeus 14.617 F-618 A, B.
58 See references in note 4.

factually a scene in a real play; and (4) though the *sileni* or **satyrs** which he is studying may be portrayed as dancing, the observer cannot be sure that they are in all cases, or in any one case, actually dancing the *sikinnis*. Further, if one does use the vase paintings, so elementary a matter as careful observation is essential. One esteemed writer,[59] describing a vase painting showing *sileni,* states emphatically that the four figures there portrayed come dancing in "mit lustigen Sprüngen." As a matter of fact, the painting, reproduced in his book, shows no leaps whatsoever. Two of the *sileni* have both feet on the ground, a third *silenus* has one leg bent at the knee, as if in a hop or a kick to the rear, and the fourth *silenus* crouches, moving forward. They seem to be carrying pieces of furniture, to the accompaniment of a flutist.

With these cautions in mind, the student of the dance will nevertheless learn much from the Greek artists.[60] He will see, e.g., dancing satyrs and *sileni* slapping or striking their own sides, backs, and thighs, or those of others; kicking forward, sideward, or to the rear; strutting impudently, with hands on hips; crouching; creeping stealthily; hopping, often over some obstacle, such as a wine cup; walking on their hands; or even riding pickaback on a comrade's shoulders. He will see a great deal of evidence of tipsiness, as, e.g., awkward leaning, off-balance, to the side or to the rear *(to opisthen kamptesthai);* violation of the normal principle of "opposition"—as, for instance, the moving of the right arm and leg forward together, instead of the right arm with the left leg, in natural balance; and drunken antics, such as the pouring of wine from a wineskin into a companion's mouth. The student also will see a frequent use of *cheir simē,* the "warding-off" figure; a gesture of the hand upon the buttocks, which calls to mind the *energeis* of the *kordax* of comedy; various other more or less obscene gestures; and the figure which the Greeks called *airein maschalēn,* a strong "lifting of the armpits," with the palms of the hands close to or flat against the body.[61] An early fifth-century clay base for a votive offering, from Skione in Macedonia,[62] shows

---

[59] Brommer, *Satyrspiele* (1st ed.; above, note 1), p. 13 and Fig. 6.

[60] See illustrations in the books listed in note 1, above.

[61] Cf. Lillian B. Lawler, "*Airein Maschalēn* and Associated Orchestic *Schēmata,*" *Transactions of the American Philological Association,* LXXX (1949), 230-237.

[62] D. M. Robinson, *Corpus Vasorum Antiquorum, U.S.A.,* Fasc. 4, "The

Silenus moving stealthily, almost slinkingly, with torso bent forward and left leg strongly flexed, and the left hand held out low in front, with fingers tense, and the right hand held before the eyes in the *skopos* gesture. Similar figures appear in other collections. A vase in New York even shows a satyr patting his stomach and the top of his head at the same time, a maneuver which calls to mind a modern children's game! In nondramatic settings the *sileni* and satyrs pursue Maenads, and brandish snakes; whether these motifs ever appeared in the dance of the satyr play we have no means of knowing.

Repeatedly, in considering the dance of tragedy, comedy, and the satyr play, we have noted steps, *schēmata*, and gestures attested for one genre recurring in the dance of one or both the others. This need not disturb us. The dramatic dance in general must have had certain common characteristics, perhaps stemming ultimately from early dances at festivals in honor of Dionysus. In tragedy these probably would have been refined and rendered symbolical, to a considerable degree; in comedy, and even more so in the satyr play, much of their original tone would have remained. Also, we must not forget that in both comedy and the satyr play there must have been much burlesque of serious things, including tragedy.

The *sikinnis* was regularly accompanied by the music of the double flute, and, to a lesser extent, the lyre. In his list of types or genres of flute music, quoted from Tryphon, Athenaeus (14.618 C) includes fourteen names, all of which have been associated with the *sikinnis* by one or another of the modern scholars who have considered this subject. Walker[63] proposed a place in the *Ichneutae* for at least six of them. The types are: *kōmos* ("revel"); *boukoliasmos* ("bucolic" or "ox-tending"); *gingras* ("fife-like");[64] *tetrakōmos* (for a tetragonal *kōmos*-dance); *epiphallos* ("phallic"); *choreios* ("suitable for a chorus"); *kallinikos* (for a processional dance of victory); *polemikos* ("warlike"); *hēdykōmos* ("sweet, charming revel"); *sikinnotyrbē* ("sikinnis-rout"); *thyrokopikon* and *krousithyron*, which Tryphon says are the same

---

Robinson Collection" (Baltimore, 1934), Part 1, Plate XLVIII and Commentary, p. 57.
[63] Walker (above, note 29), pp. 184-188.
[64] Cf. Athenaeus 4.174 F-175 A, B.

("door-knocking"); *knismos* ("the itch"); and *mothōn* ("writhing," "twisting"). Tryphon adds that all these types of music were used to accompany the dance. In the absence of any definite evidence one way or another, all that can be said with assurance is that, so far as we know, any of these types of music *might* have been used with the *sikinnis*. Many of them have been associated also with comedy and even with tragedy. After the classical period, instruments other than the flute and the lyre were undoubtedly introduced into the satyr play.

Occasionally, even in the fifth century, classical dramatists seem to have experimented by substituting for the satyr play in a tetralogy a play of a different type—a short drama, neither satyr-ic nor tragic, perhaps with a happy ending. The *Alcestis* of Euripides, as we have seen, is such an experimental play.

By 341 B.C. the rule requiring each writer of tragedy to compete at the City Dionysia with three tragedies and a satyr play began to lapse. In that year the dramatic ceremonies opened with a single satyr play; after this play, each of the three tragic poets who were competing presented three tragedies. In 340 B.C. each poet offered only two tragedies. In the third century there was a renewal of interest in the satyr play, and some of the earlier ones were re-staged. But after the third century the satyr play declined in Athens, and its character may have changed markedly. The dance in particular must have undergone considerable change. The uproarious *sikinnis*, performed by twelve *choreutae*, with unrestrained leaps and whirling turns, was, of course, entirely possible in an *orchēstra* or dancing-place sixty or seventy feet in diameter; but with the introduction into the theatre of a narrow stage in the Hellenistic period, and the transfer of all action from the *orchēstra* to that stage, either the number of the dancers must have been drastically reduced, or a more restrained type of dance must have been instituted.

After the third century B.C., the satyr play seems to have been more popular outside Athens than in that city. In Alexandria and in smaller cities throughout the Greco-Roman world, satyr plays were produced down to and, indeed, after, the time of Cicero. Horace speaks of the satyr play as being produced in Rome in the reign of Augustus. It is possible that both Greek and Roman authors by that time may have been writing satyr plays which

[124]

differed greatly from those of the Attic theatre of the best period. Unfortunately no evidence on this score has come down to us.

The satyr drama never attained the prestige and universal appeal of comedy in the Attic theatre—much less of tragedy. However, it did draw the dramatic performances back, for a time, to the Dionysiac source from which they were all said to have been derived ultimately, and it did display Greek genius in another of its many and varied aspects.

We do not know when the satyr plays ceased to be performed in the Attic theatre. It is possible, however, that even after the abandonment of the satyric drama as such the dances which were featured and brought to a characteristic height of development in the satyr play may have survived in folk festivals and private *kōmoi* down to the Christian period.

INDEX

acrobatics, acrobatic dancing, 42-43, 108-109, 120
Adonis, dances lamenting, 96
Adrastus, dances in honor of, 4, 6
Aeschylus, 22-51, 88, 93
Agathon, 61, 90
agōn, 81
agōnothetēs, 21
airein maschalēn, 35 (note 39), 78, 122
Alcibiades, 45
Alexandria, 124
"alphabet" dances, 91-92
Amorgos, dances on, 70, 100
anabolē, anabolai, 17
Anacreon, 74
"anamix" alignment, 85, 93
anapaestic meter, 26, 29, 32, 67-68 (note 8)
angelikē orchēsis, angelikon, 26
animal dances, schēmata, and mummery, 4, 15, 53, 56, 57, 65, 84-88
Anthesteria, dances at, 100
antistrophe, 11-14, 17, 28, 29, 51
Antyllus, 76
aphallesthai, 76
Aphrodite, and dances to, 40, 111. See also Venus.
apodiōgma, 89-90
apokinos, 73, 74, 80, 110
Apollo, and dances to, 21, 43, 45, 50, 53, 70, 100, 111, 114, 115, 116
Apollonia, dances at the, 21
Apollonius of Tyana, 100-101
Apollophanes, 39
apopydarizō, 76
aposeisis, 73
aposkelisai, 76
aposkopōn, aposkopos, aposkopeuōn, 44, 115
apotropaic dances and figures, 38, 64, 79, 107, 108

apoxiphizein, 38
Apuleius, 72, 101-102
Arabia, Dionysiac dance in, 53
Arcadia, 40
Archilochus of Paros, 2, 3, 5, 92
Archippus, 85, 87
Ares, dance of, 52
Argos, dances in, 49
Arion of Lesbos, 5-6
aristerostatai, 27
Aristophanes, 16, 17, 18, 19, 20, 24, 34, 35, 38, 42, 50, 56, 57, 58, 63-98, 120
Aristotle, 2, 4, 5 (note 17), 26, 63-64
arkteia, 96
armed dancers, 88, 108, 109. See also Curetes, pyrrhic dance.
armpit, lifting of, 78, 122
Artemis, and dances in honor of, 15, 40, 43, 52, 58, 65, 70, 71, 74, 79, 95, 96
Asclepius, dances in honor of, 21
askōliasmos, 96
Asia Minor, and dances in, 15, 53, 107-108
ass dances, 84-86
Athena, and dances to, 15, 40, 43, 47, 92, 93
Athenaeus, 25, 35, 36, 37, 39, 40, 41, 44, 45, 70, 72, 75, 77, 80, 82, 86, 90, 91, 106, 109, 110, 117, 119, 120, 123
Athens, Athenians, and dances of, 1, 4, 6, 7, 8, 16, 18, 20, 21, 45, 47, 56, 59, 60, 63, 64, 67, 85, 87, 91, 93, 95, 97, 98, 100, 103, 104, 105, 107, 120, 121, 124, 125
Augustus, 124
Autocrates, 71, 74 (note 37)

Bacchanals, Bacchantes, Bacchic dances, 53-55, 59, 89, 101, 113.

[126]